SHAMBHALA
CLASSICS

ZEN LESSONS

The Art of Leadership

Translated by
THOMAS CLEARY

SHAMBHALA
Boston & London
2004

Shambhala Publications, Inc.
Horticultural Hall
300 Massachusetts Avenue
Boston, Massachusetts 02115
www.shambhala.com

9   8   7   6   5   4

Printed in the United States of America
♾ This edition is printed on acid-free paper that meets
the American National Standards Institute Z39.48 Standard.
♻ Shambhala makes every effort to print on recycled paper.
For more information please visit www.shambhala.com.
Distributed in the United States by Penguin Random House LLC
and in Canada by Random House of Canada Ltd

Library of Congress Cataloging-in-Publication Data
Zen lessons: the art of leadership / translated by Thomas
Cleary.
p. cm.
ISBN 978-1-57062-883-2
1. Priests, Zen—China—Quotations.
2. Leadership—Religious aspects—Zen buddhism—Quotations,
maxims, etc.   3. Zen Buddhism—China—Quotations, maxims, etc.
I. Cleary, Thomas F. 1949–
BQ9267.Z4661   1989   88-18604
294.3′6—dc19   CIP

CONTENTS

Contents

Contents

TRANSLATOR'S INTRODUCTION

Zen Lessons is a collection of political, social, and psychological teachings of Chinese Zen (Chan) adepts of the Song dynasty, from the tenth to the thirteenth centuries.

If the Tang dynasty, from the early seventh through the ninth centuries, may be called the classical period of Chinese Zen, the Song dynasty may be called its baroque period, characterized by complexity of form and ingenious imagery with multiple meaning.

In contrast to the relatively plain and straightforward Zen literature of the Tang dynasty, Song dynasty Zen literature is convoluted and artful. This is not regarded, in Zen terms, as a development in Zen, but as a response to a more complex and pressured society and individual. The Zen adepts of Song times did not regard the reality of Zen as any different in its essence from that of classical times, but considered the function of Zen to have become complicated by the complexity of the contemporary mind and the rampant spread of artificial Zen based on imitations of a few Zen practices.

The proliferation of false Zen was stimulated by the enormous impact of real Zen on Asian civilization. After the Tang dynasty, there is hardly anywhere one can turn in Chinese culture without seeing the influence of the Zen charisma.

The ill effects of the resulting influx of insincere followers into public Zen institutions are already noted in the works of great masters of the latter Tang dynasty, and these *Zen Lessons* contain top-level notices of an even greater decline in quality of Zen institutions and followers in the Song dynasty, in spite of Zen's unparalleled prestige in cultural terms.

There is even reason to believe that the creation of new Confucian and Taoist schools using Zen methods was especially encouraged by Zen adepts because of their awareness that the original Zen Buddhist order had become seriously enervated through the attachment of worldly feelings to its forms and personalities.

From the point of Buddhist historiography, this sort of involution is predictable: a period of true teaching is eventually obscured by imitations, and even these break down into remnants with time. The *Mahāparinirvānasūtra*, or Scripture of the Great Decease, among the classical scriptures traditionally most studied by Zen adepts, outlines these phenomena very clearly.

The false ideas about Zen and Buddhism that scandals at Zen centers have both arisen from and in turn recreated in many minds within and without these centers are also predictable and have existed ever since "Zen" became consciously articulated. Almost the entire literature of Zen, in all of its astonishing variety of forms, deals with nothing but misconceptions about the reality of Zen, which is said to be extremely simple in essence though complex in function or manifestation. The apparent complexity of Zen teaching and function is due to the complexity of the human mentality, as Zen perforce acted in more intricate ways to unify the threads of the contemporary mind.

A synthetic recreation of the original mental science of Buddhism, Zen played a unique role in the history of East Asia through its creation of entire schools of religion, philosophy, literature, art, music, social studies, psychology, psychiatry, and physical education.[1]

The inner dimension of the outward history of Zen, during which it first breathed life into a new Buddhism and later revived other philosophies when that Buddhism grew aged and ill, is hardly observed by those who think in political terms, but nevertheless it is consistently emphasized by the Zen adepts themselves.

These *Zen Lessons* illustrate the art of combining ultimate and ordinary truths, using society and conduct as a way into Zen enlightenment, by the practice of constructive criticism and higher education. This was one of the original tools of Buddhism, but in many schools it had lost its edge through excessive formalization by the time the Zen Buddhists revived its original open flexibility.

Among these schools may be counted even the Complete Reality schools of Taoism and the Inner Design schools of Confucianism. The results of Zen methods applied to Taoist and Confucian classics, these schools had as profound an impact on Chinese culture as had the original Chan schools.

The classical period of Chinese Zen is usually said to have been the Tang dynasty, from the seventh through the ninth centuries. The first large Zen commune was established in the mid-seventh century under the fourth founding teacher of Zen, and countless people were said to have been awakened by the public talks of the sixth founding teacher who was founder of the so-called southern tradition. The fourth, fifth, and sixth founding teachers were all invited to be imperial teachers, and many of their spiritual descendants became teachers of leaders of Chinese society at all levels of organization, from local to imperial.

During the Tang period some of the most influential men and women on earth studied Zen on a par with some of the humblest and most obscure men and women on earth. Zen introduced a revolution in social practice that maintained its energy through centuries of opposition and corruption, and provided one of the only historical forums for unbiased social understanding as well as spiritual understanding. Zen also influenced painting and poetry, two of the most important of Chinese arts, traditionally used for emotional education and therefore of great social significance.

As noted earlier, the Song dynasty was characterized by complexity of form and multiplicity of function within its intricate, ingenious, and often ambiguous designs. Song Zen further extended its influence through the urban arts and soft sciences, but also maintained its contact with the huge countryside of China by means of the travels and retreats of Zen workers through the network of Tang dynasty relics.

Over the Tang dynasty, Buddhism, and Zen Buddhism in particular, grew to the point where there could have been no class of people or general geographical region untouched by its influence in the China of the Song dynasty. The problem was, as predicted in Buddhist scripture, that the very success of the work would eventually attract the wrong kind of people, or rather that too many people would come with the wrong aspirations. By the last century of the Tang dynasty there are already notices of Zen establishments losing their order due to the invasion of people with faulty aspirations, and by Song times the tone among the distinguished teachers is one of emergency.[2]

Put in elementary Buddhist terms, Zen establishments were originally set up to free people from the poisons of greed, aggression, and ignorance that ordinarily afflict individuals and societies to greater or lesser degrees and do not allow humankind to attain complete practical understanding of its real destiny.

According to Zen teaching, when people in positions of great responsibility in society trust Zen adepts, it may be because of the reputation Zen gained over the centuries in this enterprise, or it may be an unconscious response to the safety felt in the presence of a truly detoxified human being. In either case, the false appeared in such profusion precisely because the true was so effective.

A complication introduced by this situation was that followers of Zen, both inside and outside the Zen establishments, often had no objective means of judging the authenticity of Zen adepts. These *Zen Lessons* reflect some of the lengths to which Zen teachers and outside supporters went in order to maintain the existence of certain organizational and psychological ideas capable of stimulating accurate perception of Zen mastery under appropriate conditions.

An enormous proportion of the Zen canon uses techniques honed to perfection during the baroque period, and therefore consists in one sense largely of technical descriptions of misconceptions of Zen and human values, analyses of the major problems of human thought and behavior in individual and social life. These descriptions are like designs of the locks that bind the conditioned human mentality, and are used to unlock those locks. The results of this unlocking are popularly called enlightenment, regarded in Zen as the initiation into higher learning experiences available to humankind.

One of the major problems encountered in the dissemination of the liberative Zen arts was the usurpation of the teaching function by imitators without the genuine inner knowledge of human psychology and Zen enlightenment. The fetishism that came to surround tokens of initiation and adepthood in Zen orders was to the true Zen leaders simply a sign of trivialization, but it was enough to deceive many naive Confucian grandees who, in the words of a late Song Zen teacher, "only admired the flowers and did not take the fruit."

Traditionally, the relationship between teacher and apprentice in Zen was formalized only after a period of association in which a certain tacit recognition had taken place. When the would-be apprentice was a monk or nun, a homeless wayfarer and professional student, it was ordinarily the teacher who recognized the student; when the would-be apprentice had home, family, and social ties, the teacher awaited the student's recognition.

By the dawn of Song times, there was already a considerable degree of formalization of many aspects of Zen procedure, demanded by the large number of followers who flocked to the gates of the prestigious Zen institutions. There developed a system of public monasteries under government control, where known Zen masters were invited to teach large assemblies during summer and winter study periods.

In the original Zen communities, everyone had to work, and duties were assigned according to ability as perceived by the core of adepts guiding the community. The Tang dynasty literature has tales of certain adepts working as cooks or hospitalers for twenty years in the communities of their teachers, but in the Song dynasty there seems to have been more rotation of internal administrators of Zen establishments through the reservoir of adepts who served in the various monasteries.

Eventually the Chinese government took official control over the appointments to the higher echelons of administrative and leadership duties. Of course, it was customary for the emperor, governor, military route commander, local grandee, or whoever was legally in charge of approving appointments to monastic office to consult the communities and adepts, but there was still ample room for imposture.

Objective criticism, particularly self-criticism, is an ancient tradition in Buddhism. It would not be too much to say that critical insight was one of the mainstays of the original schools of Buddhism. One of the strengths of the authentic projection of Zen Buddhism was its impersonal pursuit of the liberating effects of this practice. Applied to social, political, psychological, and deep contemplative experiences over the centuries, this method endowed Buddhism with a profound understanding of human nature. *Zen Lessons* explores the social, political, and psychological dimensions of this understanding.

Much of the most famous Zen literature of the Song dynasty, which in fact became the classical literature of Zen, derives from the public lectures of the masters, and therefore is highly veiled due to the inherently secret nature of Zen experience. These *Zen Lessons*, in contrast, are largely derived from private teachings, and therefore are mostly explicit.

NOTES

1. There were over a dozen sects of Buddhism in East Asia directly originating from or strongly influenced by Zen, at least three schools of philosophy, several genres of literature (including vernacular literature in general), numerous brands of visual, decorative, and architectural art, music for certain instruments, and traditional and modern schools of psychology and psychiatry, including the eighteenth-century Japanese urban Mind Studies movement and the twentieth-century Japanese Morita Therapy movement. Certain forms of physical education like martial arts are also customarily associated with Zen, at least in terms of recognition of past influence, and are still used as tools for teaching in some Zen schools. Needless to say, every form of Zen activity has real, imitation, and relic forms. The great Japanese master Musō, who lived shortly after the time of these *Zen Lessons*, discusses this in his *Dream Dialogues*.

2. The sayings of Baizhang Huaihai, or Dazhi, the late

eighth- and early ninth-century teacher associated with the organization of early Zen communities in China, already contain strongly worded statements about institutional decadence at the core of that deterioration represented in the *Zen Lessons*, and provide early guidelines on the distinction between spontaneous authority and authoritarianism, one of the major problems of latter-day Zen. The famous *Admonitions* of Baizhang's successor Guishan also contains unambiguous language on the decay of the Zen order in the ninth century, and attributes it largely to insincerity, lack of self-control, ignorance, and assumption of self-importance within cliques. The *Ten Guidelines for Zen Schools* composed a century later by Fayan, one of the last of the classical masters, identifies even more elements in the decay of Zen, including cultism, imposture, schizoid tendencies, sterile intellectualism, covert nihilism, literary decadence, and illiteracy. Historically speaking, the *Zen Lessons* take up after the *Ten Guidelines* and provide a greatly detailed analysis of human psychology in its reaction to objective knowledge. Other material chronicling the decadence of Zen in the Song dynasty and efforts to keep it alive can be found in J. C. Cleary's translations of Dahui/Miaoxi's letters in *Swampland Flowers*, our translation of Yuanwu's *Blue Cliff Record*, and my translation of Wansong's *Book of Serenity*. Further material on the same subject as viewed by a Japanese pilgrim to Song China can be found in my translations of Dogen's *Shobogenzo Zuimonki* and *Shobogenzo*.

NOTES ON SOURCES

In the original Chinese, *Zen Lessons* is entitled *Chanlin baoxun*, or *Chanmen baoxun*, "Precious Lessons from the Chan (Zen) Schools." It was originally compiled in the early twelfth century by two outstanding Chinese Zen masters, Miaoxi (better known as Dahui) and Zhu-an. In the late twelfth century it was further expanded by a Zen master named Jingshan, into the form in which the text exists today. Several commentaries on the text were written in China over the next five hundred years. It was first published in Japan in 1279, about one hundred years after its recompilation.

Zen Lessons draws on the personal teachings of great Zen masters of the early Song dynasty, many from unusual sources, difficult to obtain or no longer extant, often originally available only through direct contact with the network of Chinese Zen schools. Some selections are not attributed to any written source and may have been written by one or another of the compilers, based on material derived from current oral tradition. Affording rare glimpses of the personalities of distinguished masters, *Zen Lessons* preserves a large body of special Zen lore that would otherwise have been lost to posterity.

Zen Lessons is a unique part of the enormous body of Song dynasty Chan Buddhist lore that still exists in written form. This text makes it apparent that the literature of Chan Buddhism was considerably more extensive than the massive corpus of Chan writing that is known today.

Numerous anthologies are cited in *Zen Lessons;* with the

notable exception of the massive *Tanqin Annals*, most of these collections no longer exist, and apparently all that is left of them is what is to be found in *Zen Lessons*. These sources are sometimes given abbreviated titles, sometimes referred to only by generic names. Other sources include diaries, inscriptions, and letters. They contain rare reports of famous teachers, especially selected by the original compilers for their lack of crypticism and their application to social concerns.

ZEN LESSONS

1.
Enlightened Virtue

Mingjiao said:

Nothing is more honorable than enlightenment, nothing is more beautiful than virtue. Those who have enlightened virtue have it even though they be ordinary people, while those who lack enlightened virtue lack it even though they be kings.

There were some people who starved to death in ancient times but have been admired ever since for their virtue; there were others who were kings but have been despised ever since for their lack of virtue.

So learners worry about not being imbued with virtue, they do not worry about not being in positions of power and authority.

Tanqin Annals

2.
Study and Learning

Mingjiao said:

The study of saints and sages is certainly not fulfilled in one day. When there is not enough time during the day, continue into the night; accumulate it over the months and years, and it will naturally develop. Therefore it is said, "Accumulate learning by study, understand what you learn by questioning."

This means that study cannot bring discovery without discernment and questioning. Nowadays where students go

1

there is hardly anyone who asks a question to discern people. I do not know what they will use to help their spiritual stage and achieve the benefit of daily renewal.

Jiufeng Annals

3.
Great and Small Evil

Mingjiao said:
Of the evil that people do, there is that which has form and that which has no form. Formless evil injures people, evil with form kills people. The evil that harms people is relatively small, the evil that kills people is great.

That is why "there is poison in a party, there is spear and shield in talk and laughter, there are a tiger and a panther inside the chamber, there are savages in the next alley."

Unless you are yourself a sage and nip these in the bud, guarding against them with standards of propriety, the injury they do will be considerable.

West Lake Annals

4.
Honesty

Mingjiao related the following story:
When Chan Master Dajiao was abbot of Ashoka monastery, it happened that two monks were arguing endlessly over alms. The director of monastery affairs could not stop them, so Dajiao called them to him and upbraided them in these terms:

"Once when Bao Gong was judge in Kaifeng, one of the people reported on his own initiative that someone who had

2

entrusted a hundred ounces of white gold to him had died, and when he tried to return the money to the man's family, the son would not accept it. So he asked the judge to summon the son and return the money.

"Bao Gong thought this admirably extraordinary, and called the son to talk to him. The son declined the money, saying, 'When my late father was alive, he had no white gold to entrust privately to another house.'

"Since both men, the trustee and the son, continued to firmly refuse, Bao had no choice but to give it to a monastery in the city, for unseen blessings to propitiate the deceased.

"I saw this with my own eyes. Even people in the mundane world are still able to be so aloof of wealth and look for what is right, as this story illustrates. You are Buddhist disciples, yet you are so shameless."

Finally Dajiao cast them out, according to the rule of Chan communities.

West Lake Annals

5.
A Vessel of Enlightenment

When Master Dajiao first went to Mount Lu, Chan Master Yuantong Na, seeing him once, treated him as a great vessel of enlightenment. Someone asked Yuantong how he recognized Dajiao.

Yuantong said, "This man is true to the middle way, not biased or dependent. Whether active or at rest, he is noble and dignified. Furthermore, in his study of the Way his actions are correct, and his words are simple yet logically complete. Whenever people have endowments like this, seldom do they fail to become vessels of enlightenment."

Jiufeng Annals

6.
Modesty

In 1134, Renzong, Emperor of China, sent a court messenger with a letter to Chan Master Yuantong Na, summoning him to become abbot at the great monastery Xiaozi. Yuantong claimed to be unwell and did not rise to the summons; he sent a message that Dajiao was worthy to respond to the imperial command.

Someone said to him, "The emperor shows reverence for enlightened virtue, and his benevolence covers the beautiful landscape. Why do you firmly refuse?"

Yuantong said, "I am unworthy of monkhood, and my seeing and hearing are not clear. I am lucky to rest in the forest, eating vegetables and drinking water. There was that which even the Buddhas did not do, to say nothing of others.

"An ancient philosopher had a saying, 'It is hard to live long with a great name.' I carry out the plan of contentment in everyday life, and do not trouble myself for fame or gain. If such concerns press on your mind, when would you ever be satisfied?

"Therefore the great poet Su Shi once said, 'If you know peace, then you thrive; if you know contentment, then you are rich.' "

Avoiding fame, perfecting modesty and integrity, good from beginning to end—this was realized in Yuantong Na.

biography

7.
Rules

Yuantong Na said:
In ancient times the Chan commune was established,

with rules and guidelines, to rescue those at the end of the era of imitation from the shrouds of error. The founder never knew that students in the last part of the imitation era would usurp the rules and ruin the commune.

In remote antiquity all regulated themselves, even though they lived in nests and caves; later on everyone became reckless, even though they lived in spacious buildings. Therefore it is said, "The question of safety or danger is a matter of virtue; the question of flourishing or perishing is a matter of the time."

If virtue can be applied, what is the necessity of a monastery? If the time could be relied on, what would be the use of rules?

Records of the Fields

8.

Worry and Trouble

Yuantong said to Dajiao:

The ancient saints governed their minds before sprouting, stopped feelings before confusion. In general, preparing beforehand means no trouble. Therefore "the alarm is beaten at the outer gate to deal with thugs," and preparations are made beforehand.

When the task is done beforehand, then it is easy. If you do it hurriedly and carelessly, it must be hard. The fact that the ancient sages had not a worry all their lives and not a day's trouble truly lies in this.

Jiufeng Annals

9.
A Swift Bird

Yunji Shun said to Fushan Yuan:

If you want to find out all you can about supreme enlightenment, you must be all the more firm when you become exhausted, you should be all the more vigorous as you grow old. Do not follow the vulgar to swipe fame and profit to the detriment of higher virtue.

In jade, a pure luster is esteemed, so neither red nor purple can change its character. Pine stands out in the coldest part of winter, so neither frost nor snow can wither it. Thus we know that as propriety and righteousness are what is great in the world, it is only important to be steadfast.

Should you not strengthen yourself? An ancient said, "A swift bird flies alone, a solitary mien has no companions." So it should be.

Extensive Record

10.
Work and the Way

Fushan Yuan said:

The ancients associated with teachers and selected companions, never letting themselves slack off. They were never afraid to work hard, even down to husking grain and preparing food, immersed in common labor. During my own apprenticeship I experienced this fully.

But as soon as there is any consideration of whether you will get any profit or not, as soon as there is any comparison of gain and loss, then there will be no end of wavering and compromise.

6

And if one is not personally upright and true, how could one be able to study the Way of enlightenment?

Talks of an Attendant

11.
Hot and Cold

Fushan Yuan said:

There are certainly things in the world that grow easily, but we have never seen anything that could live given one day of warmth and ten days of cold.

The supreme Way is clearly there before the mind's eye, so it is not hard to see, but it is essential to be firm of will and powerful in practice.

This should be dealt with whatever you are doing. If you believe for one day and doubt for ten, if you are diligent in the mornings but put it off at night, not only will it be hard to see the Way right before your eyes, I fear you will be turning your back on it to the end of your life.

letter to a senior student

12.
Safety and Danger

Fushan Yuan said:

Nothing is more essential to leadership and teachership than carefully discerning what to take and what to leave aside. The consummation of taking or leaving is determined within; the beginnings of safety and danger are determined without.

Safety is not the safety of one day, nor is danger the danger of one day. Both safety and danger come from gradual development.

7

It is imperative to examine the matter of leadership. To uphold leadership by means of enlightened qualities accumulates enlightened qualities, to uphold leadership with courtesy and justice accumulates courtesy and justice. Exploitative leadership accumulates resentment and enmity.

When resentment and enmity build up, inside and outside are estranged and opposed. When courtesy and justice build up, inside and outside are harmonious and happy. When enlightened qualities accumulate, inside and outside are sensitive and compliant.

So where there is a plenitude of enlightened qualities, courtesy and justice, then inside and outside are happy. When exploitation and resentment are extreme, inside and outside are miserable. It is the feelings of misery and happiness to which calamity and blessing respond.

letter to Master Jingyin Tai

13.
Three Essentials of Leadership

Master Fushan Yuan said:

There are three essentials to leadership: humanity, clarity, and courage.

Humanely practicing the virtues of the Way promotes the influence of the teaching, pacifies those in both high and low positions, and delights those who pass by.

Someone with clarity follows proper behavior and just duty, recognizes what is safe and what is dangerous, examines people to see whether they are wise or foolish, and distinguishes right and wrong.

The courageous see things through to their conclusion, settling them without doubt. They get rid of whatever is wrong or false.

Humanity without clarity is like having a field but not plowing it. Clarity without courage is like having sprouts but not weeding. Courage without humanity is like knowing how to reap but not how to sow.

When all three of these are present, the community thrives. When one is lacking, the community deteriorates. When two are lacking the community is in peril, and when there is not one of the three, the way of leadership is in ruins.

letter to Master Jingyin Tai

14.
Incompatibility

Fushan Yuan said:

Wise and foolish, virtuous and corrupt—they are like water and fire not being put in the same vessel, like cold and heat not being simultaneous. It is a matter of their natures.

The virtuous and wise are pure and refined, honest and considerate. They make their designs on the basis of enlightened virtues, humanity, and justice. When they speak out or do something, they only fear that they may not accord with people's states or not penetrate the underlying principles of things.

The corrupt are treacherous and deceitful, proud of themselves, flaunting their abilities, indulging in cravings, grabbing profit, totally heedless.

So when a spiritual community has wise and virtuous people, the virtues of the Way are practiced, comprehensive principles are established, and eventually it becomes a seat of true teaching. Let one bad one mix in among them, disturbing the group, and inside and outside will be uneasy—even if they had the original rules of Chan communes, what use would they be then?

9

The excellence and inferiority of the wise and foolish, the good and the bad, is such as this; how can we not choose between them?

a letter of Master Huili Fang

15.
Leadership and the Community

Fushan Yuan said:

The leader, who is in a position overseeing others, should be humble and respectful in dealing with subordinates. Functionaries should work wholeheartedly for the leadership. When above and below are in harmony, then the path of leadership goes through.

If the leader is proud and haughty, and subordinates are lazy and personally careless, the minds of those above and below do not communicate. Then the path of leadership is blocked.

When ancient saints served as overt leaders, they would casually have discussions with students during leisure time, touching upon just about everything. From this, one word or half a phrase is recorded in the annals, which even now we extol. What could the reason be?

One is the desire to cause higher minds to be communicated to those below, so that the Way of enlightenment is not blocked or obscured.

Second is their prior knowledge of the capabilities of students, and whether they were suitable or not.

When the saints came forth and when they withdrew, it was all in accord with what was appropriate. There was a natural respect and harmony between those above and those below, so people from far and near came to join with respect.

The rise of the Chan communities came about in this way only.

letter to Master Touzi Yiqing

16.
Vermilion Outhouses

Fushan Yuan said to Daowu Zhen:

The case of those who, while their study has not yet arrived on the Way, still flash their learning and run off at the mouth with intellectual understanding, using eloquence and sharpness of tongue to gain victories, is like outhouses painted vermilion—it only increases the odor.

Recollections of West Lake

17.
Mastering Mind

Master Yuan said to Wuzu:

Mind is the master of one body, the basis of myriad activities; if the mind is not perfectly enlightened, then delusions naturally arise.

Once delusions are born, perception of truth is not clear. When perception of truth is not clear, right and wrong are confused.

Therefore, in mastering the mind, one must seek perfect enlightenment.

When enlightened, the spirit is harmonious, the breath is quiet, the countenance is dignified, and the body is firm. Errant conceptions and emotional thinking all melt in the real mind. When you govern the mind this way, the mind will naturally be radiantly immaculate.

11

After this, if you guide people who are lost and confused, who would not follow the teaching?

True Record of Fushan

18.

Mistrust

Wuzu Fayan said:

In the monastic communes of present times, when students of the Way do not become known and are not believed by people, it is usually because their conduct is not purely good and their efforts for people are not truly appropriate. They may suddenly grab fame and profit, then show off their embellishments all over. So they are criticized by those who know.

This obscures the essential wonder of truth. Even if such people have buddhistic virtues, when heard or seen they will be doubted and mistrusted. If you have a roof over your head someday, you should remember this to make yourself work.

letter of reply from Fojian to Touzi

19.

The House of Homeleavers

Wuzu said:

When my teacher's teacher was first living at Yangqi, whose name he later made famous, the old building had broken beams and was barely enough to give shelter from the wind and rain.

One night as winter was approaching, snow and sleet

covered the benches, so that there was no place to sit. The monks earnestly asked him to let it be repaired, but the old master put them off, saying:

"Buddha said, 'In the time of the aeon of decline, even the high cliffs and deep valleys are changing and inconstant—how can you have it all completely as you wish, seeking satisfaction for yourself?' You have all left home and society to study the Way, but your way of acting is frivolous. You are already forty to fifty—how can you have leisure time to be concerned with a fine building?"

And after all he did not consent. The following day he got up in the hall and said,

"The walls of the room I lodge in have chinks, the benches are all strewn with pearls of snow. Drawing in my neck, I sigh in the dark and think back to the ancients living under trees."

Extensive Record

20.

Chan Adepts

Wuzu said:

Chan adepts guard the citadel of the mind and serve the rules of the precepts. They think of this and practice this day and night.

Their actions do not go beyond their considerations, and their considerations do not go beyond their actions; they have a beginning and accomplish its end.

Just like a plowman with field borders, rarely do they go over.

Records of Equanimity

13

21.
Chan Communities

Wuzu said:

The Chan community is a place for the molding of sages and ordinary people, and for nurturing and developing potential ability. It is a source of teaching. Even though many people are living together, gathering in kind, they are guided and made equal. Each has a transmission from the teacher.

Now in many places they do not strive to maintain the standards of the sages of the past. Biased feelings of like and dislike are many, with people bending others to what they personally think is right. How should later students take an example?

Records of Equanimity

22.
Knowing People

Wuzu said:

To help others and transmit enlightenment, it is important to find suitable people. The difficulty of knowing people is a problem for sages. You may listen to what people say, but that does not guarantee their actions. You may observe their actions, but you might miss their ability.

How can you know people unless you have been associating with them and have had a chance to examine them thoroughly from the basis to the details, searching into their resolve and practice, observing their capacity and ability, eventually to see if they can maintain the Way and conceal their function?

As for those who sell their names and adorn their appearances, they are impostors and should not be admitted. See to the depths, every hidden subtlety.

This principle of searching observation and careful listening is not something that can be done in a day and a night. That is why some of the greatest ancient adepts went through apprenticeships lasting ten or fifteen years. The cause of the transmission of the ancient sages was definitely not something that the shallow could presume to inherit and uphold. The universal guidance can be successfully continued only when there is complete mind to mind communication.

This principle of searching observation and careful listening has clear evidential proof in experience. It does not admit of clever words and commanding appearance, expedient partisanship and flattery, as satisfactory for selection.

letter of Yuanwu

23.
Virtue and Benevolence

Wuzu said:

The power of an exemplary leader lies in the practice of benevolence and virtue—it will not do to neglect one of them. If you have benevolence without virtue, people will not respect you. If you have virtue without benevolence, the people will not approach you.

If one knows benevolence attracts, and goes on to help out with virtue as well, then the benevolence which is carried out will be sufficient to settle above and below and invite people from all quarters.

If one is guided by virtues worthy of respect and goes on to help with benevolence as well, then the virtue which is upheld will be sufficient to succeed to the enlightened ones of the past and guide the ignorant and deluded.

15

Therefore a good leader nourishes virtue, thereby to practice benevolence, and spreads benevolence, thereby to uphold virtue. When one has virtue and is able to nourish it, then one is never cramped; when one has benevolence and is able to practice it, then there is gratitude.

Thus do virtue and benevolence store each other, benevolence and virtue activate each other. Thus one will be spontaneously respected yet remain approachable. What seeker of the Way would not come to such a guide? It is necessary to understand these essentials to transmit the qualities of enlightenment and promote education.

letter to Foyan

24.
Mastery in Both Worlds

When Wuzu Fayan moved from Haihui to Dongshan, Master Taiping Fojian and Master Longmen Foyan, both his former disciples, went there to pay him a visit.

Wuzu gathered the elders and advanced working monks for an evening chat.

Wuzu asked Fojian about the weather where he lived. Then he asked about the harvest from the monastery estates under Fojian's mission. As Fojian took some time to figure the yield, his old teacher Wuzu solemnly upbraided him for failing to live up to his responsibility, as evidenced by not being completely current on the status of the permanent endowment supporting the whole community.

In a letter to a younger adept of a later generation, the master Geng Longxue wrote of Wuzu, "In general, Wuzu was always stern and swift in discernment of states. Ever since Fojian had become a disciple of Wuzu, his replies were slow,

16

even to the point of being like this. An ancient said, 'When the teacher is strict, the Way studied is honored.' Therefore the fact that many descendants of the East Mountain School of Chan, that is the school of Wuzu Fayan, were outstandingly wise and virtuous, is a true case of the proverb 'When the source is deep, the flow is long.' "

25.
An Inscrutable Buddha

When Chan Master Wuzu Fayan saw monks of integrity who were worthy of promotion, in private meetings he sternly put them off and did not make any accommodations in words or attitude.

When he saw those who were prejudiced and deluded, flattering and deceitful, base in their actions, he would be extra kind and respectful to them. Nobody could fathom this.

In Wuzu's choices as to what to take and what to cast aside, there was always a reason.

Geng Longxue's postscript to Wuzu's sermons

26.
Great Light

Wuzu said:

The ancients were glad to hear of their own errors, delighted in doing good, were great in magnanimity, generous in concealing others' wrongs, humble in association with companions, and diligent in helping and saving the people. They did not defile their minds, therefore their light was great, shining through present and past.

letters of reply to Lingyun

17

27.

Essentials of Leadership

Wuzu said to Fojian:

As a leader it is essential to be generous with the community while being frugal with oneself. As for the rest, the petty matters, do not be concerned with them.

When you give people tasks, probe them deeply to see if they are sincere. When you choose your words, take the most serious. Leaders are naturally honored when their words are taken seriously; the community is naturally impressed when people are chosen for their sincerity.

When you are honorable, the community obeys even if you are not stern; when the community is impressed, things get done even if no orders are given. The wise and the stupid each naturally convey their minds, small and great each exert their effort.

This is more than ten thousand times better than those who hold on by authoritarian power and those who cannot help following them, oppressed by compulsion.

letter to Fojian, in the personal record of an attendant

28.

Worry

Wuzu said to Guo Gongfu:

The temper and feelings of people are certainly inconsistent. They shift daily, along with changes. Although Buddhism has flourished and declined repeatedly since ancient times, the reason for its thriving or degeneration has always come from the teaching activity.

In ancient times when the early Chan masters were helping people, they fanned with a clear wind, regulated with purity, covered with moral virtue, and taught propriety and right, causing students to control their seeing and hearing, to stop bad tendencies, to cut off indulgence in desire and to forget about gain and honor.

Thereby they moved daily toward goodness, put error at a distance, realized the Way and fulfilled its virtues, all without being self-consciously aware of it.

People of today are far from being like the ancients. If they want to investigate this path all the way, they must make their determination firm and unbending, until they reach enlightenment; afterward it is left to nature whether one may experience calamity or distress, gain or loss. People should not try unreasonably to escape them.

Why should anyone fail to do this because they are worried beforehand that they may not succeed? As soon as there is the slightest concern sprouting in your heart, not only will you fail to realize enlightenment in this life—you will never have a time of fulfillment.

Annals of the House of Equanimity

29.

The Self-Pointer

Baiyun said to Gongfu:

In former times Cuiyan Zhen, "the Self-Pointer," deeply savored Chan contemplations, and being eloquent and sharp of tongue, he reviled everyone, no one ever meeting with his approval.

Yet in reality the great truth was not perfectly clear to him. One day a senior student from another cloister, seeing him, laughed and said, "Elder brother, although you have

19

studied a lot of Chan, you are still not perfectly enlightened. This should be called ignorant Chan."

Evening talks of Baiyun

30.
Defeatism

Baiyun said:

How could the flourishing or decline of the Way be constant? It is just a matter of people spreading it. This is why it is said, "Putting it into practice means survival, giving it up means perishing."

So it is not that the Way is apart from people—people depart from the Way.

People of old stayed in mountains and forests, lived inconspicuously in cities and towns; they were not drawn by fame and profit, they were not deluded by sound and form. Eventually they were able to purify and order one time, and leave an excellent legacy to ten thousand generations.

Can what was possible in the past not be possible now? It is only because teaching is not complete and practice is not powerful. Some say the ancients were pure and simple, and therefore could be taught, while people of today are fickle and shallow, and therefore cannot be taught. These are actually words that foster delusion—truly they are not worthy of consideration.

letter of reply to Guo Gongfu

31.
Speech and Action

Baiyun said to the layman Yang Wuwei:

What can be said but not practiced is better not said. What can be practiced but not spoken of is better not done.

When you utter words, you should always consider their end. When you establish a practice, you must always consider what it covers.

In this, ancient sages were careful about their words and chose their acts.

When they spoke they did not just demonstrate the principle of Chan, they used it to open the minds of students who were not yet enlightened.

When they established their practices, they did not just take care of themselves, they used them to educate students who were undeveloped.

Therefore, when they spoke their words had standards, and when they acted it was with proper manners. So ultimately they were able to speak without trouble and act without disgrace. Their words thus became scriptures, their acts became standards.

So it is said, "Speech and action are the pivot of ideal people, the basis of governing one's person." They can move heaven and earth, touch even ghosts and spirits, so they should be respected.

True Record of Baiyun

32.
Seeing Through

Baiyun said to Wuzu:

Many Chan Buddhists with knowledge and ability see after something is already so, but cannot see before it is not yet so.

Cessation of conceptions, insight into objective reality, concentration, and knowledge guard beforehand. Doing, stop-

21

ping, letting go, and extinction are noticed after they have already happened.

Therefore, what doing, stopping, letting go, and extinction use is easy to see, while what cessation and insight, concentration and knowledge do is hard to know.

But the determination of the ancients was on the Way. They cut off thoughts before they sprouted. Although they had cessation and insight, concentration and knowledge, doing, stopping, letting go, and extinction, all of it was a question of process.

Therefore it is said, "If there is any talk about beginning and end, it is all self-deception." This saying is that of an ancient master who saw all the way through and did not deceive himself.

True Record of Baiyun

33.
Study without Turning Away from People

Baiyun said:

Many monks I have seen have never considered the long range. I fear that the monasteries will weaken from this. My late teacher Yangqi used to say that when those above and below try to take it easy, this is the greatest calamity for the teaching.

In the past when I was living in seclusion in the library at Guizong monastery and read through scriptures and histories, many hundreds of them crossed my eyes. The books were extremely worn and old, yet as I opened each volume I had a sense of new discovery.

As I think about the matter in these terms, study without turning away from people is like this.

True Record of Baiyun

34.
Acting Too Early

Zhantang related:

Baiyun first led the Chengtian public monastery in the Nine Rivers region, then moved to Yuantong monastery. He was very young for a Chan master.

At that time the great master Huitang was at Baofeng monastery. He said to Yue Gonghui, "The new abbot at Yuantong clearly sees through the fundamental, and does not disgrace Yangqi's succession. It is a pity, however, that he went into action too early—this is not fortunate for a monastery."

When Gonghui asked the reason, Huitang said, "Acknowledged accomplishment and excellent capacity are begrudged by Creation, and not given fully to humankind. What people strongly want, Heaven will surely take away."

When Baiyun died at Haihui, he was just fifty-six years old. This was an exceptionally early death for a Chan master. Those who know say that the great master Huitang was aware of subtle indications, a genuine man of wisdom.

Record of Things Heard by Zhantang

35.
Continuing Education

Master Huitang called on Yue Gonghui at Baofeng. Gonghui's clear understanding of the profound doctrines of the *Heroic March Scripture* was foremost in his time. Each phrase, each word that Huitang heard was like a precious jewel to him, and he was overcome with joy.

Among the monks in Huitang's community there were some who privately criticized their leader. When Huitang

23

heard of it, he said, "I sound out his strengths and work on my shortcomings—what is there for me to be ashamed about?"

Ying Shaowu said, "Master Huitang's study of the Way is a model for Chan monks. Still he considers the inherent superiority of honorable virtue to be strength, and considers what he has not yet seen or heard to be a shame, causing those in the monasteries who inflate themselves and belittle others to have a standard of which to be mindful. This is of some help indeed."

Lingyuan's Remnants

36.

Decisions

Huitang said:

It is essential to leadership that one should take the far-reaching and the great, and leave off the shortsighted and the petty. If a matter remains stubbornly unresolved, one should consult seasoned and mature people, and if there is still doubt one should question the knowledgeable. Then even if there is something unfinished, still it will not be too much.

If, on the other hand, leaders like to give free play to their own personal feelings and take or give solely by themselves, one day they will run afoul of the schemes of petty people. Whose fault is this?

So it is said, "Planning is with the many, decision is done alone." By planning with the group, one can examine the ultimate effect of benefit or harm; by deciding oneself, one can determine right and wrong for the community.

letter to Caotang

37.
Personnel Problems

One day Huitang saw the great master Huanglong with an appearance of unhappiness, and asked him about it. Huanglong said, "I haven't found anyone yet who can be the accountant for the monastery."

Huitang then recommended the assistant superintendent Gan.

Huanglong said, "Gan is still rough—I'm afraid that petty people might intrigue against him."

Huitang said, "Attendant Hua is rather honest and prudent."

Huanglong said, "Although Hua is honest and prudent, he is not as good as Xiu, the supervisor of the estate."

Lingyuan once asked Huitang, "When Huanglong needed an accountant, why did he give it so much thought?"

Huitang said, "Those with nations and those with families have always made this basic. Was it only Huanglong who was like this? The ancient sages also have enjoined this."

recorded on the wall at Tongan

38.
Graduate Studies

Huitang said to Zhu Shiying:

When I first entered the Way, I relied on myself very readily. Then after I saw my late teacher Huanglong, I retreated and considered my daily activities. There was much in them that was contradictory to principle.

So finally I worked on this for three years. Even in extreme cold and humid heat my determination was unbending. Only after that did I finally manage to accord with principle in all events.

And now, every move I make is also the living meaning of Buddhism.

39.
Sages and Ordinary People

Huitang said:

The Way of sages is like sky and earth raising myriad beings, nothing not provided by the Way.

The ways of ordinary people are like rivers, seas, mountains, streams, hills and valleys, plants, trees, and insects—each fulfills its own measure, and that is all. They do not know outside of that what is complete in everything.

But could the Way be two? Is it not that there turn out to be great and small only because of depth or shallowness of realization?

letter of reply to the layman Zhang Wujin

40.
Being in the World without Misery

Huitang said:

What has been long neglected cannot be restored immediately.

Ills that have been accumulating for a long time cannot be cleared away immediately.

One cannot enjoy oneself forever.

Human emotions cannot be just right.

Calamity cannot be avoided by trying to run away from it.

Anyone working as a teacher who has realized these five things can be in the world without misery.

letter to Master Xiang

41.
Communication of Hearts

Huanglong said:

Essential to leadership is winning the community. Essential to winning the communty is seeing into the hearts of the people. An ancient Buddha said, "Human hearts are fields of blessings for the world, since this is where the path of reason comes from."

Therefore, whether or not a time is safe or prohibitive, whether something is deleterious or beneficial, always depends on human hearts. What is in people's hearts may be communicated or blocked—thence do safety and prohibition arise. Things are done with more or less care—thence do harm and benefit come.

Only sages can communicate with the hearts of all under heaven. Therefore, in the hexagrams of *The Book of Changes*, when the sky trigram is below and the earth trigram is above, this hexagram is called safety. When sky is above and earth below, this hexagram is called prohibitive. Symbolically, decreasing above and increasing below is called prosperity, while decreasing below and increasing above is called decline.

Now if the sky is below and earth above, their positions are certainly contrary, yet it is called safety, because above and below are intermingling. If the host is above and the guest positioned below, their meanings are certainly in accord, yet

27

that is called prohibitive, because above and below do not intermingle.

Therefore when heaven and earth do not intermingle, beings are not great. If human hearts do not communicate, things are not harmonious. The meaning of decline and prosperity, harm and benefit, also come from this.

Now if those who are above other people are able to control themselves and thereby be generous with those below, those below will gladly serve those above. Would this not be called prosperity? If those above slight those below and indulge themselves, those below will surely resent and oppose those above. Would this not be called decline?

Thus when those above and below intermingle, then there is safety and peace. When they do not intermingle, something is wrong. People who lessen themselves are a benefit to others; people who aggrandize themselves are harmful to others.

How could the winning or losing of hearts be easy? Ancient sages likened the human being to a boat, heart being the water—the water can carry the boat, and it can also overturn the boat. When the water goes with it, the boat floats, and when the water goes against it, the boat sinks.

Therefore, when a leader wins people's hearts there is flourishing, and a leader that loses people's hearts is abandoned. Winning them completely means complete flourishing, losing them completely means complete rejection.

So when both are good there are many blessings, and when both are bad the calamity is severe. Good and bad are of the same kind, just like pearls on a thread; flourishing and decline happen in this pattern, clear as the sun in the sky. This is a basic guide for generation after generation.

letter to Huanglong Sheng

42.

Make the Way Wide

Huanglong said to the great statesman Wang Anshi:*

Whatever you set your mind to do, you always should make the road before you wide open, so that all people may traverse it. This is the concern of a great man.

If the way is narrow and perilous, so that others cannot go on it, then you yourself will not have any place to set foot either.

Zhang River Annals

43.

No Deception

Huanglong said:

If in your speech and silence, in what you do and what you do not do, you can say of yourself that you do not deceive heaven above, do not deceive people outwardly, and do not deceive your own mind within, this can truly be called achievement.

Yet remaining careful about the hidden and the subtle when alone, if you find that there is ultimately no deception going on at all, then this can be called achievement.

letter of reply to Wang Anshi

*Also considered one of China's great poets, Wang Anshi was a Chan practitioner and an active statesman. At the peak of his career he was highly placed and tried to institute sweeping reforms in government. He met with great resistance from entrenched interests, and was eventually ousted.—Translator

44.
The Chief Elder

Huanglong said:

The position of the chief elder is to be a vessel of enlightened qualities. When ancient sages established communes, set forth organizing principles, and set up names and ranks, choosing a renunciant with enlightened qualities for the title of chief elder, it was so that the elder would practice those enlightened qualities, not that anyone should have ambitions for this name.

My late teacher Ciming once said, "One who preserves the Way through old age to death in mountains and valleys is not as good as one who practices the Way leading a group of people in a commune."

Is it not the case that when one preserves the practice of the chief elder well, the virtues of the Way of the enlightened abide?

letter to Cuiyan Zhen

45.
Passing the Test

In private teaching, Huanglong used to give three barrier sayings, but few comprehended this device. When someone occasionally made a reply, he would just close his eyes and sit still without any particular approval or disapproval.

The recluse Pan Yanzhi inquired further about this. Huanglong said, "One who has already passed the barrier goes on freely. The one who asks the gateman whether it is all right or not is one who has not yet gone through the pass."

Book of the Forest

46.
Farther and Farther

Huanglong said:

The Way is like a mountain; the farther you climb, the higher it is. The Way is like the earth; the farther you go, the farther it extends. Shallow students use up their strength and stop. Only those who have will for enlightenment can reach its heights and depths. As for the others, who would have anything to do with them?

Record of Things Heard

47.
Will

Huanglong said to the layman Ying Shaowu:

The will should be made singleminded, unregressing, for a long time. Then someday you will surely know the ultimate goal of ineffable enlightenment.

If, on the other hand, the mind retains likes and dislikes, and your feelings indulge in prejudice, then even if you have a determined spirit like that of the ancients, I fear you will never see the Way.

recorded on a wall

48.
Adding Dirt to a Mountain

Master Baofeng Ying said:

The old abbots everywhere commenting on the sayings and teachings of the enlightened ones of old and criticizing them are adding dirt, as it were, to a mountain, pouring water into an ocean. How can they be made any higher or deeper than they are?

31

When you look into the intention of the commentators, you see that it is to add to the ancient teachings. But they do not realize themselves that they are not the ones who can do this.

Extensive Record

49.
Loss of Integrity

Ying Shaowu said to Huitang:

The whole matter of being known as a teacher and upholding the teaching in place of the Buddhas, causing mendicants to turn their minds to the Way, revising morals and changing customs, is not something that can be done by the shallow.

Monks of the last age do not cultivate virtues, and few have integrity. Time and again they bribe and curry favor, wagging their tails seeking sympathy, pursuing fame and fortune at the doors of temporal power.

One day their karma will be fulfilled and their luck will be dissipated—gods and humans will be sick of them. They will defile the true religion and be a burden to their teachers and companions. How can I not lament?

Huitang agreed.

Lingyuan's Remnants

50.
Mind and Traces

Ying Shaowu said to Pan Yanzhi:

Those who studied in ancient times governed their minds, students nowadays deal with the traces. The difference

32

between the mind and the traces is as that between sky and earth.

51.
Don't Rush

Ying Shaowu said to Master Zhenjing Wen:

Whatever is rushed to maturity will surely break down early. Whatever is accomplished in a hurry will surely be easily destroyed. What is done without making consideration for the long run, and is hastily finished, is not of a far-reaching and great character.

Now sky and earth are most miraculous, but still it is only after three years and two intercalary months that they complete their accomplishment and fulfill their transformations. How much the more so for the miracle of the Great Way—how could it be easily mastered? It is essential to build up achievement and accumulate virtue. Therefore it is said, "When you want to be quick, you don't succeed; act carefully and you won't miss."

A beautiful accomplishment takes a long time, ultimately involving lifelong consideration. A sage said, "Keep it with faith, practice it with keenness, perfect it with faithfulness— then though the task be great, you will surely succeed."

Lingyuan's Remnants

52.
The Call of Duty

When Zhenjing nominated Wayfarer Guang to be the leader of Wufeng monastery, the group protested that Guang was coarse and simple, lacking the talent to deal with people.

But when Guang held the leadership, he governed him-

33

self strictly and dealt with the community magnanimously. Before long a hundred ruins had been restored, and traveling monks all talked about it.

When Zhenjing heard of this, he said, "How can students criticize and praise so easily? I always see the critics saying, 'That leader practices the Way and takes care of the community; that leader doesn't exploit the communal endowment and suffers the same hardships as everyone.' But then for one who is known as a teacher and is leader of a community, it is a matter of course not to exploit the communal endowment and to suffer the same hardships as everyone else—how is it worthy of special mention?

"It is like when a grandee becomes a public official and takes care of the people for the nation, and says, 'I don't accept bribes, I don't harass the people.' But is the practice of not accepting bribes and not harassing the people anything beyond the call of duty?"

informal talks of Shantang

53.

Hypocrisy

Zhenjing said:

Few monks of the last age have integrity: whenever they see others' lofty conversation and broad discourse, they say to themselves that no one can equal themselves. But when they are given a meal, then they after all assist those with whom they had first differed, and praise those whom they had previously torn down.

It is hard to find anyone who will say that what is right is right and what is wrong is wrong, who is balanced, true, and upright, free from hypocrisy.

recorded on a wall

34

54.
Genuine Care

Zhenjing said:
The rule for Chan practitioners is that their lifestyle should not be luxurious and filling, for if it is there will be excess. Pleasing things should not be striven for much, because much striving ends in failure. When you try to succeed in something, something will surely be ruined.

I saw my late teacher Huanglong deal with the world for forty years, and in his speech and silence, action and inaction, he never tried to captivate students with expressions, manners, or literary skills. Only those who certainly had insight and were truly acting on reality, he would carefully develop in every way.

His care and respect were in the manner of the ancients. Rarely was there anyone in any of the Chan communities comparable to him. Therefore today as I face the community I take him as an example in everything.

diary

55.
The Use of Finery

When Zhenjing was abbot of Baoming monastery in Jiankang, the king of Shu sent him a present of plain silk. Zhenjing asked an attendant, "What's this stuff?"

The attendant said, "It's woven silk gauze."

Zhenjing said, "What's the use of it?"

The attendant replied, "It could be made into a vestment."

Zhenjing pointed to the muslin robe he wore and said, "I always wear this, and those who see do not object."

Then Zhenjing had the silk sent to the keeper of the storehouse to sell to feed the community.

diary of Li Shanglao

56.
Advice to a King

Zhenjing said to the king of Shu:

In your daily activities, vigorously carry out whatever is right and put a firm stop to whatever is wrong. You should not change your will on account of difficulty or ease. If because of today's difficulty you shake your head and pay no heed, how can you know that another day it will not be as hard as today?

diary of Li Shanglao

57.
The Just

Master Zhantang said:

Those with enlightened virtue please the people, those without enlightened virtue please themselves. Those who please the people grow, those who please themselves perish.

Nowadays many of those who are called leaders deal with the people on the basis of likes and dislikes. When we look for those who know what is bad about what they like and know what is good about what they dislike, we find that they are rare.

Therefore it is said, "Those who share the same grief and happiness as the people, the same good and bad, are the just." Who would not take refuge where there is justice?

Laike's Collection of Growths

58.

Adaptation

Zhantang said:

For wayfarers of all times, the right strategy for skillfully spreading the Way essentially lies in adapting to communicate. Those who do not know how to adapt stick to the letter and cling to doctrines, get stuck on forms and mired in sentiments—none of them succeed in strategic adaptation.

An ancient sage said, "The hidden valley has no partiality—any call will be echoed. The huge bell, stuck with the clapper, resounds every time."

So we know that advanced people who know how to get through counter the ordinary to merge with the Way. They do not fail to change responsively by sticking to one thing.

letter to Li Shanglao

59.

Selecting Associates

Zhantang said:

When you seek an associate, it should be one who is worthy of being your teacher, one whom you will always honor and respect, and one you can take for an example in doing things, so there will be some benefit in your association.

You should still follow a teacher who is just a little better than you, to be alerted to what you have not yet reached. But if a teacher happens to be equal to you, it is better not to have such a teacher at all.

True Record of Baofeng

60.
Knowing People

Zhantang said:

Someone's conduct cannot be thoroughly known for sure from one reply or one question. In general, it seems that those who are eloquent and swift of tongue cannot always be believed in fact, and those whose words are clumsy and dumb may be inexhaustible in principle.

You may get to the bottom of people's words yet fail to get to the bottom of their reason. You may silence their tongues yet fail to conquer their minds.

The difficulty of knowing people is what ails sages. This is especially true as monks in recent times who are bright do not strive to communicate with the hearts of other beings. In what they see and hear they mostly look for faults and weaknesses. They go against the desires of the community and turn away from the Path. They deceive those who esteem them, and they seek the downfall of those who overshadow them. Thus they cause the Path of enlightened teaching that has continued since time immemorial to gradually deteriorate and weaken, almost to the point where it cannot be saved.

letter to a layman

61.
Insects

Zhantang said to Miaoxi:

In the age of imitation, many outwardly follow along with things and inwardly fail to clarify their minds. Even if they do great works, they are not ultimate. In general, it is the baseness and vulgarity of the people with whom they associate that makes them that way.

It is like the case of insects: if they gather on an ox, they do not fly more than a few paces; but if they stick to a swift horse, they can chase the wind and pursue the sun, simply because of the superiority of what they cleave to.

So students should always choose carefully where they will stay, and always go with good people. Then eventually they can cut off error and bias, approach balance and right, and hear true words.

diary

62.
Loftiness of Spirit

Zhantang said to Miaoxi:

When you study Chan, it is necessary that your consciousness and thought be lofty and far-reaching, that your determination and spirit be transcendent.

When speaking and acting, keep people's faith—do not follow devious expediency for power or gain. Then naturally you will not be defined by your company, who are uplifted and downcast by the changing times.

Record of Things Heard at Baofeng

63.
Sincere Liking for Learning

Zhantang said:

Lingyuan liked to read through the classics and histories. When he read a classic or a history book, he would keep reading it until he had memorized it.

Huitang chided him about this, but Lingyuan said, "I have heard that one who uses much effort garners a far-reaching result."

39

Secretary of State Huang Luzhi, an advanced Chan student, said, "Lingyuan is as fond of learning as hungry and thirsty people are of food and drink, and he has no ambition for fame or profit. It seems to me that his sincere heart is natural and not forced."

Laike's Collection of Growths

64.
Timing

Lingyuan said to Changling Diao:

The activity of the Way certainly has its own timing. Long ago when Ciming was a vagabond he was slighted by everyone who saw him, but he just laughed. Asked why he laughed, Ciming said, "When a jewel and a pebble come in contact, you know the pebble cannot win."

Then after he saw the master Shending, Ciming's fame was heard throughout the Buddhist world. Eventually he revived the moribund Linji school of Chan Buddhism.

The Way and time—can they be forced?

a scroll

65.
Too Late

Lingyuan said to the astronomer Huang:

In ancient times someone said, "If there is fire at the bottom of a pile of brush on top of which you are reclining, as long as the fire has not reached you, you are sure it is safe."

This truly describes the workings of safety and danger, the principle of life and death. It is as clear as the sun in the sky, it does not admit of the slightest deviation.

People usually stay in their accustomed situations, rarely reflecting on the calamities of life and death. One day something will come up that they cannot fathom, and then they will sit down and beat their breasts, but all will be helpless to come to the rescue.

a hanging scroll

66.
Back to Basics

Lingyuan said to Fojian:

Anytime I have received a letter from your teacher Wuzu, he has never spoken of worldly matters. He sincerely forgets himself in spreading enlightenment, guiding and supporting those who come later.

Recently I received a letter that said, "The fields have been ruined by drought, but I am not worried. I am only worried by the fact that Chan students have no eyes. This summer there were over a hundred people, but not one of them understood the story about dogs having no enlightened nature. This is something one might worry about."

These words are sublime, are they not? If you compare him to those who worry that the temple will not be taken care of, who fear the censure of officials, who fret that their rank is not elevated, and who are afraid that they will not have many followers, he is as different from these as the sky is from earth.

record of an attendant

67.
Gradual Development

Lingyuan said:

When you cut and polish a stone, as you grind and rub

41

you do not see it decreasing, yet with time it will be worn away. When you plant a tree and take care of it, you do not see it increase, but in time it gets big.

When you accumulate virtue with continued practice, you do not see the good of it, but in time it will function. If you abandon right and go against truth, you do not see the evil of it, but in time you will perish.

When students finally think this through and put it into practice, they will develop great capacity and emanate a fine reputation. This is the way that has not changed, now or ever.

a scroll

68.
Narrowmindedness and Indulgence

Lingyuan said to Master Huigu:

Calamity and fortune depend on each other, good and bad luck are in the same city. The fact is simply that it is people who call these on themselves.

So how can you not think?

Some only consider what delights or angers themselves, and are narrowminded, or are lavishly wasteful in indulging themselves and go along with others' desires.

These are not what a leader should do—they are really a protraction of selfish indulgence, the source of the ills of excess.

a scroll

69.
Gain and Loss

Lingyuan said to the Confucian sage Cheng Yi:

Calamity can produce fortune, fortune can produce calamity. This is because when one is in situations of disaster and danger, one is earnest in taking thought for safety, and when one is deeply immersed in seeking out order, one is capable of seriousness and discretion—therefore good fortune is born, and it is fitting.

When fortune produces calamity, it is because when living in tranquility people indulge their greed and laziness, and are mostly scornful and arrogant—therefore calamity is born.

A sage said, "Having many difficulties perfects the will; having no difficulties ruins the being."

Gain is the edge of loss, loss is the heart of gain. Therefore blessings cannot visit over and over again, one cannot always hope for gain. When you are in a fortunate situation and so consider calamity, then that fortune can be preserved; when you see gain and consider loss, then that gain will surely arrive.

Therefore a superior person is one who when safe does not forget danger, and who in tmes of order does not forget about disorder.

a scroll

70.
Overreaching Oneself

Lingyuan said:

Those who overreach themselves in positions of leadership rarely finish anything successfully. It seems that their virtuous qualities are superficial and their measure is narrow, and their learning from experience is low. Also they cannot follow the good and strive for righteousness and use that to expand themselves and achieve realization.

daily record

43

71.
Be Careful

Lingyuan said:

Learners must be careful about what they take up and what they leave aside; they cannot be unthinking in what they say and do.

People of few words are not necessarily fools; glib people are not necessarily wise. Rustic, simple people are not necessarily unreasonable or rebellious; those who are servile and obedient are not necessarily loyal and true.

Therefore a teacher does not understand people's states on the basis of words, and does not select students on the basis of ideas.

Who among the mendicants in the world does not want to seek enlightenment? Yet those who are enlightened and see reality are hardly one out of a hundred or a thousand. Even those who are cultivating themselves and diligently practicing, storing learning and planting virtue, need thirty years to accomplish it. If there happens to be one thing wrong and the communities reject you, then you can never be established in all your life.

Even jewels that light the way for a chariot cannot be flawless, even a gem worth many cities cannot be free from defect. How can there be no faults in ordinary beings with feelings? Even Confucius, who was a sage, still said he studied *The Book of Changes* for fifty years before he became free from gross errors.

A scripture says, "Do not fear the arising of thoughts, just beware of being slow to become aware of it." How fitting this is—for who since the sages has ever been free from error?

It is a matter of one who really knows developing it completely—then the being is not wasted. So it is said,

"Skillful carving is a function of following curves and angles; whether crooked or straight, there is no wasted material. Good riding is in the proper way of meeting situations of danger and ease; neither the slow nor the swift lose their nature."

Since things and animals are like this, so should people be. If you follow sentiments of like and dislike in your actions, leave those who are different from you and join those who are like you, this is due to laying out curves and lines without string and marker, or assessing weight without a balance. Although you may have a fine touch, you cannot be entirely free from error.

72.
Good Leadership

Lingyuan said:

Good leaders make the mind of the community their mind, and never let their minds indulge in private prejudices. They make the eyes and ears of the community their eyes and ears, and never let their eyes and ears be partial.

Thus are they ultimately able to realize the will of the community and comprehend the feelings of the community.

When they make the mind of the community their own mind, good and bad are to the leaders what good and bad are to the community. Therefore the good is not wrongly so, and the bad is unmistakably so.

Then why resort to airing what is in your own mind, and accepting the flattery of others?

Once you use the community's ears and eyes for your ears and eyes, then the people's perceptivity is your own— thus it is so clear nothing is not seen, nothing not heard.

So then why add personal views and stubbornly invite hypocrisy and deception from others?

When they expressed their own hearts and added their own views, the accomplished sages were striving to find their own faults, to have the same wishes as the people of the community, and to be without bias.

Therefore it is said that for the wide spread of virtue, humanity, and justice, it is appropriate to be that way. Yet those with ignorant and impure minds strive to find others' faults, differing in their wishes from those of the community, sunk in personal prejudices. Therefore none of the people fail to become estranged from them. And therefore those whose bad name and perilous deeds are told far and near also must be like this.

By this we know that when leaders have the same desires as their communities, they are called wise sages. When their desires differ from those of their communities, they are called mediocre.

In general, there is a difference in the meanings of opening up and offering one's views—good and bad, success and failure, go in opposite ways like this. Can it not be the difference in the sentiments with which they seek fault, and the dissimilarity in the ways in which they entrust people?

73.
Two Winds

Lingyuan said:
Those acting as chief elders in modern times are often seen to be unclear in their knowledge when involved in two conditions. Touched by two winds, they lose the substance of the teaching.

One of these conditions is adverse circumstances, in which most are touched by the wind of decline. The second condition is favorable circumstances, in which most are touched by the wind of gain.

Once you are touched by these two winds, the breaths of joy and anger mix in your heart, and looks of depression and moodiness show in your face. This brings disgrace on the teaching and vilifies the sages.

Only the wise can turn circumstances into methods of teaching, beautifully guiding the later generations. For example, when Master Langya went to Suzhou, he happened to receive donations amounting to over a thousand strings of cash. He sent people to count it secretly, had money sent anonymously to monks in the city monasteries, and the same day provided a feast for the community.

Langya himself, meanwhile, made his preparations and left before dawn the next day. At dawn, the community realized he was gone. Some followed him to Changzhou and got to see him, returning after obtaining the benefit of the teaching.

Seeing Langya made people develop faith and plant the seeds of the Way more deeply. This is what is called turning circumstances into a way of teaching. This is quite different from those who steal religious rank for their own personal profit.

a letter

74.
The Obvious and the Unknown

Mr. Fan Wenzhang said to Chan Master Langya:

Last year when I came here I wanted to find someone from the Chan Buddhist community worth talking to. I asked an official whether there were any good monks in the mountains, and he praised two monks named Xi and Mao, who lived in a temple in the north.

I asked, "Are there no others beside these two among the meditators and disciplinarians?"

The officer said, "Confucians esteem the conduct of gentlemen, monks talk about virtuous action. As for these two men, Xi and Mao, they have not crossed the threshold of the temple for thirty years, they only wear plain muslin, and they are not concerned with becoming famous or getting anything for themselves. Therefore the local people esteem their practice and honor them as teachers. But whether they are of those who actually teach as the Buddha did with freedom of mind and masterful eloquence, to be known as true guides, this is not within my power to know."

When I had some free time I went to visit Xi and Mao, and saw that their conduct was just as the official had said. I retired and reflected how these regions have been praised for their good way of life since long ago. Now as I see that old official, even he could distinguish superior people from petty people—how much the more can those who really know!

Master Langya said, "What the official said was truly lofty—please record it to educate the unlearned."

Separate Record of Langya

75.

Beyond the Range of Arrows

Lingyuan said:
Master Yuan of Zhongshan never associated with nobles all his life, and did not grasp fame or profit. He governed himself with humility, and enjoyed himself with the Way.

When grandees started urging him to become a public teacher, Yuan said, "If you have a good field, why worry that it will mature late? The only thing to fear is lack of ability and equipment."

A grandee who heard of this said, "Birds fly away on seeing men of foreboding countenance, and gather after flying beyond the range of arrows. So it is with Master Yuan."

Laike's Collection of Growths

76.
Commitment

Linyuan said:

An ancient teacher said, "In studying the Way, realizing it is hard; once you have realized it, preserving it is hard. When you can preserve it, putting it into practice is hard." When you are going to carry out the Way, this is even more difficult than realizing and preserving it.

Generally speaking, realization and preservation are a matter of diligent effort and firm perseverance, striving on your own alone; but practice necessitates an equanimous mind and a lifelong commitment to lose yourself and help others.

If the mind is not even and the commitment is not firm, then loss and benefit will be backward, and you will degenerate into a common mundane priest—this is something to beware of.

77.
An Inimitable Teacher

Lingyuan said:

Wuzu Fayan was extraordinary by nature. He was balanced in speech and silence, and whenever he said anything his reasoning was naturally overwhelming. When others tried to imitate him, they were either weird and vulgar or wild and crude; ultimately no one could match him. One like him could not be found even among the ancients.

Nevertheless, he guided people with more humility than that of a hungry and thirsty man. He once said, "I have no teaching—how can I encourage disciples? I am a true criminal in this school."

78.
Self-Examination

Lingyuan's study of the Way and application of its principles was pure and sincere, rich in virtue. He had the air of the ancients. He was peaceful and serious, and spoke little. He was very much honored and respected by scholars and grandees. He once said,

"What the people take lightly and are careless of, the sage is careful with. In particular, to be the leader of a community and assist the process of enlightenment is impossible unless one's action and understanding are in mutual harmony.

"The essential thing is repeated self-examination and self-criticism, not letting thoughts of fame and profit sprout in the mind.

"If there is anything not believed in among the directives of the teachings, anything the students do not obey, then one should withdraw to consider and cultivate virtue, waiting until a way comes.

"I have never seen anyone who was personally upright whose community was not orderly. Truly in this lies the meaning of the saying 'Looking upon the countenance of a virtuous person clears people's minds.' "

Record of Things Heard

79.
Storage and Development

Lingyuan said to Yuanwu:

If Chan practitioners who have the sustenance of seeing the Way nevertheless fail to store and develop it profoundly and richly, when they go into action it will inevitably be sharp and rough. This will not only fail to assist the teaching, it will also, I fear, incur trouble and disgrace.

80.
Sincerity and Truthfulness

Chan Master Yuanwu said:

The study of the Way is in truthfulness, the establishment of truthfulness is in sincerity. Only after you can maintain inner sincerity can you free people from confusion; by maintaining truthfulness in yourself you can teach people to shed delusions. Only truthfulness and sincerity are helpful without drawbacks.

So we know that if sincerity is not whole, the mind cannot be safeguarded or trusted. If truthfulness is not whole, one's words cannot be acted upon. An ancient said, "Food and clothing can go, but truth must not be lost."

So a guide should teach people with sincerity and truthfulness. If one's heart is not sincere and one's acts are not truthful, how can one be called a guide?

The Book of Changes says, "Only when ultimate sincerity prevails in the world can nature be fulfilled." The ability to fulfill nature means to be able to fulfill human nature. If one cannot fulfill oneself and yet expects fulfillment of others, the people will surely be deceitful and uncooperative. If one is not sincere beforehand and yet speaks of sincerity afterward, the people will surely doubt and will not trust. This is the meaning of the saying "When you shave hair, you should get it down to the skin; when you cut nails, you should cut them down to the flesh."

Truly if sincerity is not complete, people are not moved by it. If there is no decrease, there will be no increase. All in all, it is quite clear that sincerity and truthfulness cannot be dispensed with for a moment.

letter to Government Inspector Wu

81.
Correcting Faults

Yuanwu said:

Who has no faults? To err and yet be able to correct it is best of all. Since time immemorial, all have lauded the ability to correct faults as being wise, rather than considering having no faults to be beautiful. Thus human actions have many faults and errors—this is something that neither the wise nor the foolish can avoid—yet it is only the wise who can correct their faults and change to good, whereas the foolish mostly conceal their faults and cover up their wrongs.

When one changes to what is good, virtue is new every day. This is characteristic of what is called the ideal person. When one covers up one's faults, the evil is more and more manifest. This is characteristic of what is called the lesser person.

So it is that the ability to follow what is right when hearing of it is considered difficult from the standpoint of ordinary feelings. To gladly follow good when seeing it is what is esteemed by the wise and virtuous.

I hope you will forget about the outer expression of the words.

letter to Wen Wangbu

82.
The Phoenix and the Wolf

Yuanwu said:

My late teacher said that among those who serve as chief elders there are those who move people by enlightened virtue and those who make people obedient by the power of authority. It is like the phoenix in flight, which all the animals like, or tigers and wolves stalking, which all the animals fear. As far as being moved and being obedient are concerned they are one, but the types are as different from each other as the sky is from the earth.

Laike's Collection of Growths

83.
Winning People

Yuanwu said to Librarian Long:

If you want to order a community but do not work at winning people's hearts, the community cannot be ordered. If you work on winning people's hearts and do not take care to make contact with those in the lower echelons, people's hearts cannot be won. If you try to make contact with those in the lower echelons but do not distinguish the good from the bad, then those below cannot be contacted.

In trying to distinguish good people from bad, if you dislike it when they say you are wrong and like it when they follow you, then good and bad cannot be distinguished.

Only the wise adepts do not dislike to hear how they are wrong and do not delight in having others go along with them. Only the Way is to be followed, and this is how people's hearts are won and how communities are ordered.

Extensive Record

53

84.
The Community Mind

Yuanwu said:

Leaders make the knowledge of the community their knowledge, they make the minds of the community their mind. They are always wary of failing to comprehend the feelings of even one person, or failing to apprehend the principle of even one thing.

Leaders should only seek what is good, diligently striving to seek and take advice. They should question right and wrong in principle regardless of whether the matter is great or small. If the principle is right, even though it involves great expense to carry it out, what is the harm? If the thing is wrong, even though it is a small measure to get rid of it, what is the loss?

The small is a step of the great, the subtle is the sprout of the obvious. This is why the wise are careful of the beginning, sages are mindful of warnings. Even dripping water, if it does not stop, can ultimately turn a mulberry orchard into a lake. A flame, if not removed, will ultimately burn a meadow.

When the water is streaming and the fire is raging, the disaster is already happening—even if you want to help, there is no way. Of old it has been said, "If you are not careful about minor actions, ultimately they will encumber great virtue." This is what is meant here.

letter to Fozhi

85.
Leadership and Pride

Yuanwu said to Yuan Budai:

In fulfilling the role of a leader assisting the spread of the Buddhist teaching, always be thinking of giving help and salvation, and practice this without pride. Then many will be those reached and many those saved.

However, if you have pride in yourself and an inclination to flaunt your abilities, then thoughts of ambition arise and an impure mind results.

engraved in stone at Shuanglin

86.
Beginning and End

Yuanwu said to Miaoxi:

In whatever you do, you should be careful about the ending and the beginning. What is done well inevitably turns out well, and what starts well finishes well. If you are as careful of the end as of the beginning, then there will be no failure.

As the ancient saying goes, "What a pity that the robe yet unfinished is turned into a shirt. The hundred-mile journey is still halfway at ninety." This expresses lament at having a beginning without an end. So it is said, "Anyone may begin something, but few can bring it to a conclusion."

In the old days my spiritual uncle Huitang said, "Master Huangbo Sheng was indeed an extraordinary monk, but he erred later in life. As he was when he began, could he not have been called wise?"

Yunmen Hermitage Collection

87.
Precedents

Yuanwu said to Fojian:

Our spiritual grandfather Baiyun always considered the

ancients in whatever he did. He once said, "If a matter is not referred to in ancient precedents, it is called unlawful. First being acquainted with many sayings and deeds of past sages, one can then accomplish one's will."

But it is not a matter of special liking for antiquity—it is simply that people of today are not sufficient as examples. My late teacher always used to say that his teacher held to the old and did not know the changes of the times, but the old teacher said, "Changing the old and the constant is the big trouble of people today, and I will never do it."

diary of Master Chan

88.
Election

When Master Fojian moved from Taiping monastery to Zhihai monastery, the provincial governor Ceng Yuanli asked him who could succeed to the leadership of Taiping.

Fojian mentioned the assembly leader Ping. The governor wanted to see him, but Fojian said, "Ping is a strong and upright man, remote from mundane concerns and free from desires; even if you ask him to be abbot, still I think he may not go along. How could he agree to come on his own?"

The governor insisted on summoning him, but Ping said, "Then I would be a self-promoted leader," and finally ran away to Mount Sikong. The governor said to Fojian, "No one knows a son like his father."

Then the governor bade all the major public monasteries to insist on the invitation to Ping to be the leader of the Taiping community, so he could not avoid it anymore and acceded to the order.

diary of Attendant Zhan

89.

The Best People

Fojian said to Shun Fodeng:

The most excellent people do not consider fame and position to be prosperity, and those who arrive at the truth are not troubled by oppression or devastation.

To exert one's strength when seeing there is favor to be gained, or to offer one's services when seeing there is profit in it, is the behavior of mediocre and lesser people.

diary

90.

Mind and Environment

Fojian said to Assembly Leader Ping:

Anyone called a chief elder should not crave anything at all, for as soon as one craves anything one is plundered by outside objects. When you indulge in likes and desires, then an avaricious mind arises. When you like getting offerings, then thoughts of striving and contention arise. If you like obedient followers, then petty flatterers will join you. If you like to score victories, then there is a gigantic rift between yourself and others. If you like to exploit people, then voices of resentment will be heard.

When you get to the bottom of all this, it is not apart from one mind. If the mind is not aroused, myriad things spontaneously disappear. Nothing I have ever realized in my life goes beyond this. You should be diligent and set an example for future students.

engraved on stone at Nanning

91.
Frugality

Fojian said:

My later teacher Wuzu was frugal; he had one bowl pouch and one shoe bag, mended a hundred times, repaired a thousand times, yet he still could not bear to discard them.

He once said, "These two things accompanied me as I left my village hardly fifty years ago—how could I throw them away halfway along the road?"

A certain elder monk sent him a robe of rough cloth, which he said he had gotten from overseas and which was supposed to be warm in winter and cool in summer. My late teacher said, "When it is cold I have firewood for embers and paper for covering. When it is hot there is the breeze in the pines, there are water and stone. What should I keep this robe for?" And after all he refused it.

diary

92.
Deep and Shallow

Fojian said:

My late teacher Wuzu said that his teacher Baiyun was always open and clear, without any defensive facades. Whenever he would see some duty that should be done, he would jump up and lead the way. He liked to bring out the wise and able, and disliked those who joined and left people for opportunistic reasons. He sat upright all day in a single chair, untrammeled by anything.

He once said to an attendant, "To keep the Way, resting at ease in poverty, is the basic lot of the wearer of the patchwork robe. Those who change their devotion because of destitution or success, gain or loss, are simply not yet worthy of talking to about the Way."

diary

93.
Lasting Peace

Fojian said:

If you do not trouble for the Way, then you cannot keep your mind steadfast for long; if you are always in a condition of ease, then your determination in action will not be great. The ancients experienced difficulty and hardship, and encountered perils and obstacles, and only after that did they obtain lasting peace.

It seems that when the task is difficult the will is sharp; hardship makes the thoughts deep. Eventually one can turn calamity into fortune, turn things into the Way.

I have seen many students who pursue things and forget the Way, who turn away from the light and plunge into darkness. Meanwhile they dress up their own inabilities and fool people who consider themselves wise. They emphasize the shortcomings of others to revile people and consider themselves above them. They deceive people in this way, but they do not know there are enlightened predecessors who cannot be deceived. They blind people in this way, but do not know there is a common sense that cannot be covered up.

Therefore those who consider themselves wise are considered fools by others; those who exalt themselves are demeaned by others.

Only sages are not like this. As it is said, 'Matters are diverse and inexhaustible; ability is bounded and has an end.' If you want to try to range over unlimited matters by means of limited knowledge, then your perception will have some bias and your spirit will have an exhaustion point; therefore you will surely have some lack in the Great Way.

a letter

94.

Conduct

Fojian said:

What is to be valued in a spiritual leader is purity of conduct, maintaining great faith whereby to deal with people who come to learn. If there is anything crude and undignified in oneself left unremedied, eventually it will be spied out by petty people, and then even though one may have enlightened powers comparable to those of the ancients, still students will doubt and mistrust.

informal talk of Shantang

95.

The Air of the Ancients

Fojian said:

Of Foyan's disciples, only Gaoan is extraordinary, far beyond the state of ordinary people. He does not indulge in likes, he does things without partiality. He is pure and dignified, respectful and discreet. From start to finish he stands on his own with honor and morality. He has the air of the ancients; among the mendicants of recent times there are hardly any comparable to him.

a letter

96.
Considered Action

Master Foyan Yuan said:

One's demeanor when facing the community should be sobered while at leisure, one's words to guests should be made dignified when speaking to familiars.

When people in the Chan communities speak or act, whatever they say or do they should assess and consider first and then act on it, not being hasty or crude.

If you cannot decide for yourself beforehand, you should ask experienced elders about it. Ask widely of the wise ones of the older generation, in order to broaden your knowledge and amend your shortcomings, to shed light on what has not yet dawned on you.

How could you vainly make a show of authority, just indulge in self-esteem, showing your own ugliness? If you act mistakenly to begin with, even a hundred good things cannot cover it up in the end.

a letter

97.
Culture

Foyan said:

Human beings are born between heaven and earth, receiving the polar energies that form them. Unless they appear in the world in accord with reality, riding on the power of the vow of compassion, their desire for gain seems to be impossible to quickly eliminate.

Even sages know they cannot get rid of people's desire for gain, so they first rectify their minds by morality, and then civilize them with humanity, justice, culture, and knowledge, in order to guard against this. Over a period of time they cause people's desire for gain not to supersede their humanity, justice, culture, and knowledge, and thus complete their morality.

a letter

98.
Rules

Foyan said to Gaoan:

The overall design of the original rules for Chan communes was to show what is correct, to rein what is wrong, to provide a model and equalize the community, thus to govern the feelings of those of later generations, according to the times.

Human feelings are like water, guidelines and manners are like a dam. If the dam is not strong, the water will burst through. If human feelings are not governed, they will be self-indulgent and wild. So to get rid of feelings and end delusion, to prevent evil and stop wrong, we cannot forget guiding regulations for a moment.

But how can regulations and manners completely inhibit human feelings? They too are steps to assist entry into the Way. The establishment of guidelines is as clear as the sun and moon—those who look upon them do not get lost; it is as broad as the highway—those who travel on it do not get confused. The establishments of the sages of former times were different, but when you go back to the source you find there is no difference.

Among the Chan communities of recent times, there are those who vigorously employ regulations, there are those who stick to regulations to the death, there are those who slight regulations—all of them have turned away from the Path and have lost the principle. What brings this all about is indulging feelings and pursuing what is wrong. They never think of the ancient sages who rescued the final age from its decadence, preventing loose and indulgent states of mind, stopping cravings from the outset, cutting off the road of error and bias—that is the reason for the establishments.

East Lake Annals

99.
Slogans

Foyan said:

Students should not get bogged down in words and sayings. Generally speaking, relying on the words and sayings of others to formulate your understanding blocks the door of your own enlightenment, and you cannot get beyond verbal symbols.

In ancient times, when Da Guanpi first saw Master Shimen Cong in private interviews, he exercised his eloquence, but Shimen said to him, "What you say is words on paper—you have not seen into the essential pure subtlety of your mind. You should seek ineffable enlightenment; when enlightened, you stand out beyond, you do not ride on words or stick to phrases, you are like a lion roaring, so that all the beasts tremble with fear. Then when you look back on the study of words, it will be like comparing ten to a hundred, like comparing a thousand to a myriad."

Record of Things Heard at Longmen

100.
See Yourself

Foyan said to Gaoan:

One who can see the tip of a down hair cannot see his

own eyebrow, one who can lift thirty thousand pounds cannot lift his own body. This is like the student who is bright when it comes to criticizing others but ignorant when it comes to self-knowledge.

Collection of the Real Herdsman

101.
Recognizing a Teacher

Master Gaoan said:

When I first saw Master Fojian, I heard him speak in these terms at an informal gathering:

"Greed and hatred are worse than plunderers—oppose them with wisdom. Wisdom is like water—when unused it stagnates, when stagnant it does not circulate, and when it does not circulate, wisdom does not act. What can wisdom do about greed and hatred then?"

Although I was young at the time, in my heart I knew he was a true teacher, and so I finally asked to be allowed to stay there.

True Record of Yunju

102.
Balance

Gaoan said:

What students should keep in mind are balance and truthfulness; then even though thwarted in a hundred ways they will remain serene and untroubled.

But if they have any inclination or bias, and spend the days and nights in petty striving with gain as their aim, I fear their enormous bodies will not fit between heaven and earth.

Collection of the True Herdsman

103.
Habit

Gaoan said:

Virtue, humanity, and righteousness do not belong to the ancients alone; people of today have them too, but because their knowledge is not clear, their study is not broad, their faculties are not pure, and their wills are weak, they cannot carry them out with power, and eventually they are diverted by what they see and hear, which causes them to be unaware of their state. It is all due to delusive conceptions and emotional thinking, piling up into a deep accumulation of habit that cannot be eliminated all at once. This is the only reason that people today do not reach the ranks of the ancients.

a letter

104.
The Bequest of Extravagance

When Gaoan heard that life was extravagant at Jinshan while Cheng Gumu was leader there, he deeply lamented this, saying, "The norm of mendicants values unencumbered austerity—how could it be proper to act like that? How could anyone who for no reason conveys luxurious habits to the later generations, increasing insatiable demands, fail to be ashamed before the ancients?"

Collection of the True Herdsman

105.
The State of the Community

Gaoan said:

The great body of the leader has the community for its

65

house: distinctions are made appropriately, disbursal is suited to the vessel, action is concerned with the principles of peace and well-being, gain and loss are related to the source of the teaching. How could it be easy to be a model for people?

I have never seen a leader who was lax and easygoing win the obedience of mendicants, or one whose rules were neglected try to prevent the Chan communities from becoming barbaric and despised.

In olden times, Master Yuwang Shen sent his chief student away, Master Yangshan Wei expelled his attendant. These cases are listed in our classics, and are worthy of being taken as standards. Nowadays everyone follows personal desires, thus ruining the original guidelines for Chan communes to a great extent.

People nowadays are lazy about getting up, and many are deficient in manners when they congregate. Some indulge shamelessly in their appetite for food, some create disputes in their concern for getting support and honor.

It has gotten to the point where there is nowhere that the ugliness of opportunism does not exist. How can we ever have the flourishing of ways to truth and the full vigor of spiritual teaching that we look for?

Longshan Collection

106.
What Are You Doing?

It is related that while Gaoan was leader of the community at Yunju, whenever he saw students who failed to comprehend his devices in private teaching, he would take them aside and upbraid them in a most serious manner, saying, "Your parents nourished your body, your teachers and companions formed your mind. You are not oppressed by hunger or cold, you do not have to toil on military campaigns. Under these conditions, if you do not make a dedicated effort to accomplish the practice of the Way, how can you face your parents, teachers, and companions?"

There were students who wept on hearing the words of the enlightened teacher. This is how correct and strict his order was.

Anecdotes of Qiean

107.
The Influence of Conduct

When Gaoan was leader of the community at Yunju, he would grieve and lament when he heard any of the students were ill and had been moved to the life-prolonging hall, as if it were he himself that were ill. Morning and night he would ask about their health, and he would personally heat medicine and boil gruel for them, not giving it to them until he had tested it himself. If the weather was chilly, he would rub their backs and say, "Do you have enough clothing on?" When it was hot, he would look into their faces and ask if they were too warm.

If unfortunately anyone were too ill to save, Gaoan would not ask what the student had or did not have, but would perform all funerary rites according to what was at hand in the treasury.

Once when one of the monastery officers refused to make such an expenditure, Gaoan upbraided him, saying, "In ancient times the founder of the Chan commune established the treasury for the sake of the aged and infirm. You are not sick and not dead."

People of discernment from all quarters esteemed Gaoan's

personal conduct highly. When he retired from Yunju and went to Mount Tiantai, about fifty students followed him. Those who were unable to go wept as they parted with him. This is how much his virtue moved people.

informal talk of Shantang

108.
Retirement Home

When Gaoan retired from the leadership of Yunju, Master Yuanwu wanted to repair the Reclining Dragon Hermitage, which Foyan had built, to make a place for Gaoan to rest.

Gaoan said, "If a man of the forests has the delights of truth, the physical body can be ignored. I am seventy years old, and am now like the morning star or dawn moon—how much time can I have left? In the Lu hills of the western mountains, where the mountain forests and rocky springs adjoin, are all suitable places for me to retire in my old age—why should I necessarily have my own place before I can enjoy it?"

Before long he took his staff and went to holy Mount Tiantai, and later died on Flower Peak there.

Collection of the True Herdsman

109.
Education

Gaoan said:

There are no wise or foolish students—it is just a matter of the teacher refining them to bring out virtuous actions in them, testing them to discover their potential abilities, bringing them out and encouraging them, to give weight to their words, taking care of them to make their practice complete. Over long months and years, the name and the reality will both grow rich.

All people have the spirit—it is just a matter of careful guidance. It is just like jade in the matrix—if you throw it away, it is a rock, but if you cut and polish it, it is a gem. It is also like water issuing from a spring; block it up and it makes a bog, open a deep channel for it and it becomes a river.

So we know that in the ages of imitation teachings and remnant teachings, it is not simply that intelligence is lost or unused—there is also something lacking in the way of education and upbringing.

When the Chan communities were fully flourishing, the people in them were the leftovers of the final age of Buddhism. Those who remained in decadence were fools, while those who took responsibility for their own development were wise. That is why I say that everyone has the spirit, only it takes careful guidance.

Therefore we know of the abilities of students and the ups and downs of the times, that they will peak if treated well, be exalted if encouraged, decline if oppressed, and die out if denied. This is the basis of the dissipation or development of the virtues and capabilities of students.

letter to Commander Li

110.
Great Teaching

Gaoan said:

Nothing is more important for greatness of the teaching activity than virtue and propriety. If the leader honors virtue, the students will value reverence and respect. If the leader acts properly, the students will be ashamed to be greedy and competitive.

If the leader is at all lax and thereby loses face, then the students will become scornful and rowdy, an impediment to them. If the leader gets into a dispute and loses composure, then the students will be quarrelsome, a calamity for them.

The sages of old had prior knowledge, and eventually chose illumined knights of wisdom to be leaders of the Chan communities, to cause people who beheld them to be transformed without even being instructed.

That is why when the great ancient adepts' teaching of the Way was flourishing, outstanding people appeared. Their conduct was gentle and fine, harmonious, orderly, and peaceful. Thus should be those whose every word or indication could be guides for later generations.

a letter

111.

Expectations

Gaoan said:

My late teacher once said, "When I set out on my pilgrimage, at many of the small temples I came to there were things that were not as I thought they should be. Then when I recalled that some of the greatest of the ancient masters met their teachers unexpectedly in the informal environment of a local temple, I no longer felt vexed."

Record of Things Heard

112.

Nothing to Be Ashamed Of

Gaoan was inwardly and outwardly upright and strong. His character was stern, and he was always proper in his

70

manners. When he was a student, he was attacked and maligned time and again, but he never gave it a thought. All his life he bore himself with simplicity and modesty.

In private teaching he did not give careless approval. If there was any discord, he would deal with it soberly, in direct terms. All the students believed in him and accepted his teaching.

He once said, "My study of the Way is not greater than that of others. It is just that I have never done anything to be ashamed of in my heart."

113.
Beyond the Reach of Monks

When Gaoan was abbot at Yunju monastery, when he saw a monk attacking another's hidden faults, he would casually admonish the attacker in these terms: "The fact is not like this. For people in a monastery, the Way alone is urgent business, along with self-cultivation. How can you arbitrarily indulge in likes and dislikes, slandering other people's actions?" This is how careful and thoughtful he was.

At first Master Gaoan had not accepted the abbacy at Yunju, but the elder master Foyan sent him a letter urging him to do so. The letter said:

"Yunju is a leading monastery in the area; there you may settle the community and carry on the Way. It seems you should not insist on refusing."

Gaoan said, "Ever since there have been monasteries, the students who have had their morality ruined by this kind of name have not been few."

The elder master Fojian, hearing of this, said, "Gaoan's conduct is beyond the reach of monks."

Record of Things Heard

71

114.
Signs of Good Government

When Master Xuetang was leading the community at Qianfu, one day he asked a recent arrival where he had come from. The student said he had come from Fujian. Xuetang said, "Did you see any good leaders along the way?"

The student said, "Recently I passed through such-and-such a province, and although I have never met him, I know Master Ben of Poshan there to be a good leader."

Xuetang said, "How do you know he is good?"

The monk said, "When you go into the monastery there, the paths are clear, the halls are in good repair, there are always incense and lamps burning in the shrines, morning and night the bell and drum are sounded precisely and clearly, the morning and noon gruel and rice are clean and wholesome, and the monks are polite when they see people as they go about their activities. This is how I know Ben is a good leader."

Xuetang smiled and said, "Ben is surely wise, and you have eyes, too." He then reported these words to the governor of the prefecture and added, "I am getting old, and I ask you to invite Ben to be leader here at Qianfu, in hopes of the prosperity of the work of the Chan community."

Annals of East Lake

115.
Insidious Destruction

Xuetang said:

An iron dyke a thousand miles long leaks through ant-hills. The beauty of white jade is lost in a flaw. The supremely subtle Way is beyond iron dykes and white jade, yet greed and resentment are greater than anthills and flaws.

The essence of the matter lies in the will being true and sober, the practice being progressively refined, the perseverance being firm and sure, the cultivation being completely purified. After that it is possible to benefit oneself and benefit others.

Annals of East Lake

116.
Iron Face Bing

Xuetang said:

When I was the leader of the community at Longmen, Iron Face Bing was leader of the community at Taiping. Someone told me that when Bing was first going on study travels, before he had been gone from his native place for long he suddenly took the notes of what he had heard from the teacher who had instructed him and burned them all to ashes one night. During that time, whenever he received a letter, he would throw it to the ground and say it was just uselessly disturbing people's minds.

Annals of East Lake

117.
Inner Mastery, Outer Rectitude

Xuetang said to Master Huaian Guang:

When I was young I heard these words from my father: "'Without inner mastery one cannot stand, without outward rectitude one cannot act.' This saying is worth practicing all your life; in it is summed up the work of sages and saints."

73

I remembered these words and cultivated myself while living at home. Even now, when I am leader of a group, these words are like the balance stone weighing heavy and light, the compass and rule determining square and round. Without this everything loses its order.

Extensive Record

118.
Someone of Perception

Xuetang said:
When Gaoan addressed the assembly, he would always say, "In a group you must know when there is someone with perception." I asked him the reason for this, and Gaoan said, "Have you not read the words of Guishan, 'In your actions, take your examples from the superior, do not lazily follow the mediocre and the vulgar'? Those who while daily in the midst of the crowd do not sink into low folly all utter such words.

"In a multitude of people, the vulgar are many, the knowers are few. The vulgar are easy to get used to, the knowers are hard to get near to.

"If you can develop your will so that you are like one man facing a thousand enemies until the power of vulgar habits are ended, you will truly be transcendent, beyond measure."

Extensive Record

119.
Reflection

Xuetang said to Master Qiean:
In managing affairs one must weigh the heavy and the light; when speaking out one must first think and reflect. Strive to accord with the middle way, do not allow bias.

Hasty and careless actions seldom bring success. Even if you can get done in this way, after all you cannot complete anything totally.

When I was in the community of students, I fully witnessed benefit and harm. Only those of virtue moved people by their magnanimity. I hope those in the future who have willpower will practice this carefully. Only this will be of sublime benefit.

Lingyuan used to say, "Usually when people always dwell in inner reflection, they are able to clearly understand much, but when they get involved in things, running outside, then they oppose integration and lose the body of reality."

If you really want to think of inheriting the responsibility of the enlightened teachers, I direct you future descendants to always examine and criticize yourselves.

Extensive Record

120.
A Wearer of the Patchwork Robe

It is related that when Master Yingan Hua was the exemplar of the community at Miaoguo monastery, the elder master Xuetang used to visit him every day.

Some were critical of Xuetang for this, but he said, "My spiritual nephew Hua does not delight in gain or strive for fame. He does not prefer praise to criticism, he does not act agreeable and conciliatory for gain, and he does not put on a false face or use clever words. Add to that the fact that he sees the Way perfectly clearly, and can go or stay at will—there you have a wearer of the patchwork robe such as is hard to find. Therefore I respect him."

Anecdotes of Qiean

121.
Energy and Will

Xuetang said:

When students' energy is greater than their will, they become small, petty people. When their will masters their energy, they become upright, true people. When their energy and their will are equal, they become enlightened sages.

Some people are stubbornly hostile and will not accept any guidance for admonition—it is their energy that makes them thus. Upright and true people, even if strongly compelled to do what is not good, will remain undivided and constant to the death—it is their will that makes them thus.

Extensive Record

122.
Persecution

Xuetang said:

When Lingyuan was the leader of the Chan community at Taiping, he was unjustly persecuted by a certain government official. Lingyuan wrote a letter to our late master Wuzu, saying, "It is getting to be impossible to carry out the Way straightforwardly, and it is not my wish to be a leader by being crooked. It is better for me to set my mind free among the thousand crags and myriad ravines, living each day on straw and millet, and thus pass my remaining life. Why bother anymore?"

Before ten days had passed, there was a petition for Lingyuan to become leader of the community at Huanglong. He took this opportunity and moved.

Record of Things Heard by Assembly Leader Ting

123.
Human Figures

Xuetang said:

Lingyuan liked to categorize mendicants by comparisons. He quoted an old saying: "It is like making human figures of clay and of wood. When making a figure in wood, the nose and ears should at first be big, while the mouth and eyes should at first be small, for the craftsman may get them wrong, and then the ears and nose, being big, can therefore be made smaller, while the mouth and eyes, being small, can therefore be made bigger.

"When making a human figure in clay, the ears and nose should at first be small, the mouth and eyes at first big. Then if the craftsman should go wrong, the ears and nose, being small, can be made bigger, while the mouth and eyes, being big, can be made smaller."

Lingyuan said, "Though this saying may seem trivial, it can be used as a similitude of the great. If students making choices in face of events do not tire of 'thinking it over thrice,' after that they can be called people rich in sincerity."

Record of Things Heard

124.
A Life of Freedom

Xuetang said:

Wanan accompanied Gaoan to holy Mount Tiantai. When they returned, Wanan told me that there was an elder Deguan there, who had been secluded in a crag for thirty years, during which his shadow had never never the mountain. Mr. Long Xuetan, the district magistrate and a practitioner of Chan

Buddhism, offered a special welcome to Deguan to become abbot of Ruiyan monastery, but Deguan declined with a verse:

For thirty years alone, I've closed the door;
How can an ambassador's message reach the green mountain?
Stop trying to use the trifling affairs of the human world
To exchange for my life of freedom in the forest.

The invitation was sent again, but in the end Deguan never went to the monastery. Mr. Long admired him and likened him to a present-day Yinshan, one of the ancient eremitic masters.

Wanan also said there was an old-timer there who could remember Deguan's words: "Failing to comprehend the Way, getting excited on encountering objects, stirring thoughts along with feelings, having a wolfish heart and foxlike mind, flattering and deceiving people, cleaving to authorities, agreeing in order to flatter, pursuing fame and grabbing profit, turning away from the real, pursuing the false, turning back on enlightenment and joining the dusts—people of the Way in the forests do not do this."

Anecdotes

125.

Rich and Noble

Xuetang was born in a rich and noble house, but he had no manner of hauteur or extravagance. He kept himself moderate and frugal, he was refined and unconcerned with material things.

Once someone presented Xuetang with an iron mirror, but Xuetang gave it away, saying, "The valley stream is clear enough to reflect even a hair or a whisker—what should I keep this mirror for?"

biography

126.
Learners and Dilettantes

Xuetang was humane and compassionate, sincere and sympathetic. He revered the wise and honored the able. Jokes and mundanities rarely issued from his mouth. He was not aloof or inaccessible, nor did he act in a harsh or angry manner. In his actions he was most steadfast and pure.

He once said, "When the ancients studied the Way, they were indifferent to outside things and did away with habitual cravings, until they thus got to the point where they forgot about authority and rank, and left the realm of sound and form. They seemed to have capabilities without study.

"Students now exert all their cleverness but in the end are helpless. Why is this? If the will is not firm and the task not unified, you will just be a dilettante."

biography

127.
Self and Others

Master Sixin related:

Yuantong Xiu once said, "If one cannot be upright oneself and yet wishes to make others so, that is called lapse of virtue. If one cannot be respectful oneself and yet wishes to make others so, that is called violation of propriety. If someone working as a teacher lapses from virtue and goes against

79

propriety, what can be used to extend guidelines for the future?"

letter to Lingyuan

128.
Not in the Forefront

Sixin said to the lay student Chen Rongzhong:

If you want to seek the Great Way, first rectify the mind. If you have any anger you will not be able to rectify the mind, and if you have any craving you will not be able to rectify the mind.

However, who but saints and sages are able to be free from like and dislike, joy and anger? You just should not put these in the forefront, lest they harm rectitude—that is considered attainment.

Extensive Record

129.
The Quickest Shortcut

Sixin said:

The quickest shortcut to entry into the Way consists of moderation and relinquishment. I see many students with minds excited and mouths stammering, all eager to succeed to the Chan ancients, but I do not find one in ten thousand when I look for those with relinquishment and moderation. They are like sons of a family in society who are not willing to read books but want to be officials—even a little Confucian boy knows this is impossible.

Extensive Record

130.
Sincerity and Trustworthiness

Sixin said to Caotang:

For the task of leadership, sincerity and trustworthiness are essential in speech and action. If your words are sincere and trustworthy, the impression they make will be deep. If your words are not sincere or trustworthy, the impression they make will be shallow.

Insincere words and untrustworthy deeds are intolerable even in ordinary life in the mundane world, lest one be slighted by the people—how much more so when acting as the leader of a community, expounding the teaching of the enlightened ones. If you lack sincerity and trustworthiness in what you say and do, who in the world would follow you?

True Record of Huanglong

131.
Materialism and the Way

Sixin said:

Profit seeking has nothing to do with the Way, seeking the Way has nothing to do with profit. It is not that the ancients could not combine them, but that their forces do not accord.

If profit seeking and the Way went together, why would the ancients have given up their wealth and status, forgotten about achievement and fame, and mortified their bodies and minds in empty mountains and great swamps, drinking from streams and eating from trees all their lives?

If you must say profit making and the Way can both be carried out without mutual interference, that is like holding a

81

leaking wine cup to pour on a burning pot—you cannot save it this way.

a letter

132.
Impartiality

It is related that when Master Sixin was leader of the community at Cuiyan monastery, he heard that Master Jiaofan had been banished from the continent, and that he was passing through the region of Cuiyan on the way to his place of exile on the southern island of Hainan. Sixin sent a party to meet Jiaofan and bring him back to the monastery, where Sixin treated him cordially as a guest for several days and saw him off reluctantly.

Some people, noting that he had criticized Jiaofan in the past, said that Sixin was inconsistent. Sixin said, "Jiaofan is a virtuous wearer of the patchwork robe. In the past I used extreme words to remove the ostentation of his excellence. Now that he has run into foul play, this is his lot. I treat him according to the usual principles of the Chan communities."

Those who know say that Sixin acted in this manner because he had no partiality in regard to people.

Records of West Mountain

133.
Nature

Sixin said to Caotang:

My late teacher Huitang said, "Openness and affability in people are gotten from nature—if you try to force them, they will not last long. One who is forceful but not enduring will be treated with scorn and contempt by petty people.

"In the same way, false and true, good and evil, are also

gotten from nature, and none of them can be changed. Only people with balanced nature, who can deal with the higher and the lower, are worth associating with and teaching."

True Record

134.
Feelings

Master Caotang Qing said:

The tire that burns a meadow starts from a little flame, the river that erodes a mountain starts drop by drop. A little bit of water can be blocked by a load of earth, but when there is a lot of water it can uproot trees, dislodge boulders, and wash away hills. A little bit of fire can be extinguished by a cup of water, but when there is a lot of fire it burns cities, towns, and mountain forests.

Is it ever different with the water of affection and attachment and the fire of malice and resentment?

When people of old governed their minds, they stopped their thoughts before they came up, stopped their sentiments before they arose. Therefore the energy they used was very little while the accomplishment they reaped was very great.

When feelings and nature are disturbing each other, and love and hatred mix and conflict, then in oneself it will harm one's life, and in relation to others it will harm their beings. How great is the peril, beyond salvation.

a letter

135.
Discerning Feelings

Caotang said:

There is essentially nothing to leadership but to carefully

83

observe people's conditions and know them all, in both upper and lower echelons.

When people's inner conditions are thoroughly understood, then inside and outside are in harmony. When above and below communicate, all affairs are set in order. This is how leadership is made secure.

If the leader cannot minutely discern people's psychological conditions, and the feeling of those below is not communicated above, then above and below oppose each other and matters are disordered. This is how leadership goes to ruin.

It may happen that a leader will presume upon intellectual brilliance and often hold to biased views, failing to comprehend people's feelings, rejecting community counsel and giving importance to his own authority, neglecting public consideration and practicing private favoritism—all of this causes the road of advance in goodness to become narrower and narrower, and causes the path of responsibility for the community to become fainter and fainter.

Such leaders repudiate whatever they have never before seen or heard, and become set in their ways, to which they are habituated and by which they are veiled. To hope that the leadership of people like this would be great and far-reaching, is like walking backward trying to go forward.

letter to Shantang

136.
Natural Selection

Caotang said to Master Ru:

My late teacher Huitang said, "In a large community, the virtuous and the corrupt are together, because of the greatness of the teaching; and so one cannot but draw near to some and avoid others. It is only a matter of a little more refined selection."

If there are people with ability and virtue who meet with the expectations of the community, you should not estrange them because of personal ire. And if there are people with ordinary perception whom the community dislikes, you should not be friendly with them because of personal liking. In this way the virtuous advance on their own, the corrupt regress on their own, and the community is at peace.

If the leader indulges in personal feelings and only goes by private liking or resentment in promoting or demoting people, then the virtuous will be restrained and silent, while the corrupt will struggle forward in competition. The constitution of the institution is disordered, and the community is ruined.

This selection is truly the great body of the living exemplar. If you can sincerely examine and practice this, then those near at hand will rejoice, and those far off will tell the story. Then why worry about the Way not being carried out or seekers not coming?

carved on stone at Sushan

137.
Controlling Bias

Caotang said:

There is nothing special to leadership—essentially it is a matter of controlling the evils of biased information and autocracy. Do not just go by whatever is said to you first—then the obsequities of petty people seeking favor will not be able to confuse you.

After all, the feelings of a group of people are not one, and objective reason is hard to see. You should investigate something to see its benefit or harm, examine whether it is appropriate and suitable or not; then after that you may carry it out.

True Record of Sushan

138.
Objectivity

Caotang said to Shantang:

In all things, if right and wrong are not clear, you must be careful. When right and wrong are clear, you should decide on the basis of reason, consider where the truth lies, and settle the issue without doubt. In this way, you cannot be confused by flattery and cannot be moved by powerful argument.

Pure Spring Annals

139.
Heart-to-Heart Communication

Shantang said:

Snakes and tigers are not enemies of buzzards and vultures—buzzards and vultures follow them and screech to them. Why? It is because they have vicious hearts. Cows and hogs are not driven by magpies and jackdaws—the magpies and jackdaws gather and ride on them. Why? Because they do not have vicious hearts.

Once when an ancient Chan master visited a hermit, he found the hermit setting out half-cooked rice. The master said, "Why do crows fly away when they see a man?" The hermit was at a loss; finally he put the same question back to the Chan master. The master said, "Because I still have a murderous heart."

So those who suspect others are suspected by others; those who forget about people are also forgotten by people. The ancients who were companions of serpents and tigers had realized this principle well. One ancient said, "An iron ox does not fear the roar of a lion—it is just like a wooden man seeing flowers and birds." These words take this principle to its consummation.

letter to a layman

140.
Government

Shantang wrote to a high government official:

A rule for governing subordinates is that favor should not be excessive, for if it is excessive they will become haughty. And authority should not be too strict, for if it is too strict they will be resentful.

If you want favor without haughtiness and authority without resentment, then favor should be given to those with merit, and not given to people arbitrarily. Authority should be exercised where there is wrongdoing, and should not be wrongly brought to bear on those without offense.

In this way, though favor be rich, the people will not become haughty, and though authority be strict, the people will not become resentful.

If, on the other hand, you richly reward those whose merit is not worthy of elevation, and severely punish those whose offense is not worthy of blame, then eventually you will cause small people to give rise to hauteur and resentment.

letter to Ministry President Zhang

141.
The Mean

Shantang said:
The Way of the enlightened is not beyond finding the mean. Exceeding the mean is bias and error. Not everything in the world can fulfill your wishes, so trying to fulfill your wishes means trouble and confusion.

Many are the people of past and present who are immoderate and imprudent, in peril to the point of being in danger of destruction. So then who has no excesses? Only people of wisdom and attainment reform them unstintingly; this is extolled as excellence.

letter to a layman

142.
Peace amid Violence

Chan Master Shantang fled to Yunmen hermitage along with Ministry President Han Zicang, Chan Master Wanan, and one or two other Chan adepts, to avoid the violence of a civil war in the early 1130's. Mr. Han asked Wanan, "Recently I heard you were captured by soldiers of the rebel leader Li Cheng. How did you contrive to escape?"

Wanan said, "I had been captured and bound, and starved and froze for days on end, until I thought to myself that I would surely die. Then it happened that there was a snowfall so heavy that it buried the building and caused the walls of the rooms where we were held to collapse. That night over a hundred people were lucky enough to escape."

Mr. Han said, "At the time you were captured, how did you handle it?"

Wanan did not reply. Mr. Han asked him again, pressing him for an answer.

Wanan said, "How is this even enough to talk about? People like us study the Way: we take right for sustenance and have only death. What is there to fear?"

Mr. Han nodded at this.

So we know that our predecessors had immutable will, even in the midst of mortal calamity and trouble in the world.

Collection of the True Herdsman

143.
Who to Elect

When Chan Master Shantang retired from leadership of the community at Baizhang, he said to the government officer Han Zicang:

Those who advanced in ancient times had virtue and responsibility. Therefore they would go only at the third invitation and leave with one farewell.

Of those who advance nowadays, only those with strength who know when to go forth and when to withdraw without losing the right way can be called wise masters.

Record of Things Heard

144.
Impartiality

Shantang said to Yean:

The attitude of a leader must be impartial. In doing things, you should not necessarily consider what comes from yourself to be right while considering others wrong. Then like and dislike regarding difference and sameness do not arise in the mind. Then the breath of crass self-indulgence and mis-begotten prejudice has no way to enter.

Phantom Hermitage Collection

145.

Examples

Miaoxi said:

The ancients would adopt what was good when they saw it, and if they made a mistake they would change it. Following virtue and cultivating accord, they wanted to escape without fault. They worried about nothing so much as not knowing their own bad points, and liked nothing so much as learning of their mistakes.

Were the ancients like this because of insufficiency of intelligence, or because their perception was not clear? In truth it was an admonition to those of later times who would try to aggrandize themselves and belittle others.

The expansion of a community, with people from all quarters, is not something that can be achieved by one person alone—it is necessary to be assisted by the ears, eyes, and thoughts of associates, in order to fully comprehend what is right and to know the people's feelings and conditions.

If one rests on high rank, taking oneself seriously, being fastidious about minor tasks but slighting the great body of the community as a whole, not knowing who the wise are, not perceiving who are no good, not changing what is wrong, not following what is right, acting arbitrarily as one pleases, without any deference, this is the foundation of calamity. How could one not beware?

Should it actually turn out that there are none among one's associates worth consulting, one should still take examples from sages of the past. If you shut everyone out, you cannot quite "let in the hundred rivers to become an ocean."

letter to Master Bao

146.
Nominees

Miaoxi said:

In nominating leaders for public study communities, it is imperative to nominate those who preserve the Way and are peaceful and modest, who when nominated will grow stronger in will and integrity, who will not ruin the community finances wherever they go but will fully develop the community and also be master of the teaching, rescuing the present day from its decadence.

As for wily deceiving tricksters who have no sense of shame and, knowing how to flatter and wait on authority, cleave to powerful upper-class families, why should they be nominated?

letter to Zhu-an

147.
Common Sense

Miaoxi said to the lay student Chaoran:

In all the world, common sense alone cannot be abandoned. Even if it is suppressed and not carried out, how can that affect common sense?

This is why when someone truly enlightened is elected to lead a spiritual community, all who see and hear are joyful and praise the election. If someone unsuitable is elected, the people sadly lament the election.

In reality it is nothing but a matter of whether common

sense is carried out or not. By this you can figure out whether a Chan community will flourish or decline.

Ke-an's Collection

148.
Misrepresentation

Miaoxi said:

The ancients first chose those with enlightenment and virtue, then recommended those with ability and learning, to advance in their time.

If one who is not a good vessel is placed before others, most who see and hear will slight him, and due to this monks will think to themselves of polishing their reputation and merit to become established.

Recently we have seen the Chan communities decline as students are heedless of the virtues of the Way and lack integrity and humility. They slander the pure and plain as being crude simpletons, and praise the noisy dilettantes as being smart.

Therefore the perceptions of newcomers are not clear. They go hunting and fishing to extract and copy in order to supply themselves with eloquent remarks and sayings, getting deeper into this as time goes on, until it has become a decadent trend. When you talk to them about the Way of the sages, they are as blind as if they had their faces to the wall. These people are just about impossible to help.

letter to Zicang

149.
A Memorial

Miaoxi said:

In the old days Huitang wrote in a memorial of Huanglong: "Those engaged in this study in ancient times dwelt on cliffs and in caves, ate roots and fruits, wore hide and leaves. They did not concern their minds with fame or gain, and did not register their names in the government offices.

"Since the Wei, Jin, Qi, Liang, Sui, and Tang dynasties (third to ninth centuries C.E.), when sanctuaries were first built for assemblies of students from all quarters, the good have been chosen to regulate the corrupt, causing the wise to guide the foolish and deluded. Because of this, guest and host have been established, above and below have been distinguished.

"Now when people from all quarters are gathered in one sanctuary, it is truly difficult to bear the responsibility. It is essential to unify the great and discard the petty, to put the urgent first and the casual later, not to scheme for oneself but to concentrate on helping others. This is as different from selfish striving as the sky is from earth.

"Now the names of the successive generations of leaders at the Huanglong sanctuary are being inscribed on stone, to cause those who come later to see, look at them, and say who had virtue, who was benevolent and righteous, who was fair to the whole community, and who profited himself.

"Can we not beware?"

stone inscription

150.
The Quality of Candidates

The government minister Zhang Zishao said to Miaoxi:

The position of assembly chief in a Chan community is a rank for which the virtuous and wise are to be chosen, but nowadays in many places there is no question as to whether the assembly chief is good or bad. All use this post as a steppingstone for their ambitions. This is also the fault of the teachers of the communities.

Now in the age of imitation, it is hard to find anyone suitable for this post. If you choose those whose practice is a bit better and whose virtue is a bit more complete, who are modest and upright, then that would be a bit better than choosing those who rush ahead precipitously.

Kean's Collection

151.
Division of Responsibilities

Miaoxi said:

When the ancient worthies served as leaders of Chan communities, they did not manage the community property personally, but entrusted it to the direction of monastic officers. Chan abbots in recent times presume to extra ability and power, and refer all affairs great and small to the abbot, while the officers just have empty titles.

If you want to try to manage the affairs of a whole community by means of the capacities of just one person, keeping the people informed and keeping the general order undisturbed, would that not be hard?

letter to Shantang

152.
Exile of a Master

Wanan said:

When our late teacher Miaoxi began teaching as the leader at Jingshan, in an evening gathering he discussed Chan teaching as it was carried out at various places throughout the land. When he came to the teachings of the moribund Cao-Dong school of Chan, he talked on and on.

The next day, Assembly Chief Yin, who was a master of the Cao-Dong school, said to the teacher, "Helping people is a serious matter. One must want to help activate spiritual teaching; one should save it from decadence, according to the times, not grasp immediate convenience. When you discussed various teachers in the past when you were a Chan follower, even then it could not have been arbitrary—how much less now that you are a public teacher."

The teacher said, "Last night's talk was just one occasion."

The assembly chief said, "The study of saints and sages is based on nature—how can you slight it?"

The teacher bowed his head and apologized, but the assembly chief kept talking endlessly about the matter.

Later, when our late teacher Miaoxi was banished, an attendant recorded the statement of his exile and posted it in front of the communal hall. The monks were weeping and sniveling like people who had lost their parents, lamenting sadly, unable to rest easy. Assembly Chief Yin went to the community quarters and said to them, "The calamities and stresses of human life are something that cannot be arbitrarily avoided. If we had Miaoxi be like a sissy all his life, submerged in the rank and file, keeping his mouth closed, not saying anything, surely this exile would not have happened. But do I need to say that what the sages of yore had to do did not stop at this? Why are you bothering to aggrieve yourselves? In olden times several sincere students banded together to see the great teacher Fenyang; they ran into military operations going on in the northwest at the time, so they changed their clothes and mixed in with the battalions to make their way up to Fenyang. Now the place of Miaoxi's exile is not so far from here, there are no gaps or obstacles in the road, the mountains and rivers are not steep or forbidding—if you want to see Miaoxi, what is so hard about that?"

From this the whole crowd became silent. They next day they left in a continuous stream.

Lushan Collection of the Forest of Wisdom

153.
Criticism

Wanan said:

When my late teacher Miaoxi was exiled, there were some among the students who made private criticisms. Assembly Chief Yin said, "In general, when criticizing and talking about people, you should seek to find where the faulty are faultless—how can you find the faultless faulty? If you do not look into people's hearts, and just doubt their actions, what help is that to the democracy of the community?

"Miaoxi's virtue and capacity come from nature. In bearing and conduct he only follows duty and right, in thought and judgment he definitely excels other people. Now that Creation is putting him down, there must be a reason; how can we know but that it will be a blessing for the teaching another day?"

Those who heard this did not criticize any longer.

Forest of Wisdom Collection

154.
Safety in the Community

Assembly Chief Yin said to Wanan:

One who is known as a teacher should cleanse mind and

heart, and receive people from all quarters with utmost impartiality and uprightness.

If there is one among them who embraces the Way and is virtuous, humane, and just, you should advance that person even if there is enmity between you.

And if there is anyone who is a crooked misanthrope, you must put that person at a distance even if you are privately indebted to the person.

This will cause everyone who comes there to know what to stand by, so all are of one mind, with the same virtue. Then the community is safe.

letter to Miaoxi

155.
Making a Community Flourish

Assembly Chief Yin said:

Few are the leaders who can succeed in making a community flourish. This is because most of them forget truth and virtue and give up benevolence and duty, abandoning the regulations of the Dharma and going by their personal feelings.

Sincerely considering the decline and disappearance of spiritual schools, one should make oneself true yet humble to others, pick out the wise and good for mutual assistance, honor those of long-standing virtue, be distant from petty people, cultivate oneself with moderation and frugality, and extend virtue to others.

After that, for those whom you employ as assistants, retain those who are more mature, and keep away the opportunistic flatterers. The value of this is that there will be no slander of corruption, and no disruption by factionalism.

Forest of Wisdom Collection

97

156.
Troubles

Assembly Chief Yin said:

The sages of ancient times were wary when they had no troubles, saying, "Could Heaven have abandoned the bad?"

A philosopher said, "Only a saint can be free from troubles inside and out. Unless one is a saint, when at peace one must be anxious within."

People of wisdom and understanding know that trouble cannot be escaped, so they are careful in the beginning to guard themselves against it.

So when human life has some worry and toil, it may turn into happiness for a whole lifetime. After all, calamity and trouble, slander and disgrace, could not be avoided even by ancient sage-kings, much less by others.

letter to Miaoxi

157.
Charades

Wanan said:

Recently we see the Chan communities lacking mature people. Wherever you go there are hundreds of people, one acting as master, the group as associates. With one occupying the rank of spiritual monarch, taking up its regalia, they fool each other. Even though charlatans give speeches, they have no basis in scripture. That is the way it is—there are no mature people.

Unless one has clarified the mind and arrived at its basis, and acts in accordance with this understanding, how could one presume to teach in the Buddha's stead? It would be like someone falsely declared emperor—he brings about his own execution. Spiritual monarchy is even more serious than worldly monarchy—it cannot be taken arbitrarily.

The sages are ever more distant, while those convinced of their own school of thought are ever more ubiquitous, causing the teaching of the sages of yore to go into submergence day by day. As Confucius lamented, "I would like to say nothing, but can I?"

I set forth one or two items that have been most deleterious in crippling the Way and degrading the teaching. I have done this to circulate in the Chan communities, to let the younger generation know that their predecessors struggled hard and worked hard, with the bearing of the great teaching in their minds, like walking on ice, running on swords, not in a quest for honor or gain.

If those who understand me fault me for this, I have nothing to say about it.

Forest of Wisdom Collection

158.
Grandees and Chan Teachers

Wanan said:

Recently I have seen grandees, provincial inspectors and governors, enter the mountain cloisters, take care of official business, and then the next day have an attendant take word back to the chief elder of the Chan cloister, "Today you should give a lecture especially for such and such an official." This situation calls for reflection.

Although it is true that such instances have been recorded in books since ancient times, in every case it was the grandee who came seeking the teacher, while the Chan elder, on the occasion of the visit, would briefly mention the ideas of external protection of the teaching and glorification of nature.

99

Once grandees had become disciples, the Chan elders would tell a few light stories of the school to engender respect in them. There are well-known cases of distinguished Confucian grandees seeking out Chan masters for instruction—do you think this was particularly irrational behavior, bringing on laughter from the knowledgeable?

159.
Authoritarianism

Wanan said:

When the ancients were going to hold private meetings, they would first hang out a sign to that effect, and each individual would come bounding forth because of the greatness of the matter of life and death, eager to settle doubts and determine what is so.

In recent times we often see community leaders making everybody come and submit to them respectfully in private interviews, without question of whether they are old or sick.

If there is musk, it is naturally fragrant—what need is there to publicize it? By this they wrongly create divisions, so guest and host are not at ease. Teachers should think about this.

160.
Chan History

Wanan said:

The Chan founder transmitted both the teaching and the robe of succession. After six generations, the robe stopped being transmitted. Those whose action and understanding corresponded were taken to continue the work of the school

over the generations. The Chan path became ever more reful-
gent, with increasingly numerous descendants.

After the sixth patriarch of Chan, the great masters
Shitou and Mazu were both true heirs. The profound words
and marvelous sayings of these two great men circulated
throughout the land, and from time to time there were those
who personally realized their inner meaning.

Once there were many teachers' methods, students did
not have one sole way open, as the original stream of Chan
branched out into five, square or round according to the vessel,
the essence of the water remaining the same. Each branch had
an excellent reputation, and strived diligently to carry out its
responsibilities. So Chan communities sprouted up all over,
not without reason.

Henceforth the communities would respond and expound
back and forth to each other, revealing the subtleties and
opening up the mysteries, sometimes putting down, sometimes upholding, in this way and that assisting the process of
the teaching. Their sayings were flavorless, like simmering
board soup and cooking nail rice, served to those who came
later, for them to chew on.

The practice that evolved from this is called bringing up
the ancients. Verses on ancient stories began with Fenyang;
then with Xuedou, shortly thereafter, the sound was widely
broadcast, and he revealed its essential import, in its oceanic
boundlessness.

Later authors ran after Xuedou and imitated him, not
considering the issues of enlightenment and virtue, but striving for vividness and freshness of literary expression, thereby
causing later students of subsequent generations to be unable
to see the ancients' message in its pristine purity and whole-
ness.

I have traveled around to Chan communities, and I have

seen those among my predecessors who do not read anything but the sayings of the ancients and do not practice anything but the original pure rules for Chan communes. Is it that they particularly like ancient things? No, it is simply that people of present times are not sufficient as models. I hope for people of comprehension and realization who will understand me beyond the words.

161.
Some Bad Habits

Wanan said:
Recently we see students fondly clinging to prejudiced views, not comprehending people's conditions, shallow in faith, recalcitrant, liking people to flatter them, admiring those who follow them while estranging those who differ from them. Even if they have one bit of knowledge or half an understanding, yet it is covered by these kinds of bad habits. Many are those who grow old without attainment.

Forest of Wisdom Collection

162.
A False Teaching

Wanan said:
In the Chan communities wherever you go there is a false teaching rampant, saying that discipline, meditation, and knowledge are unnecessary, and that it is unnecessary to cultivate virtue or to get rid of craving. Talk like this is not only creating harm to the Chan communities in the present day, it is actually the bane of the teaching for ten thousand ages.

102

Ordinary people have cravings, they love and hate and desire, they are selfish and ignorant, their every thought is attached to things, like bubbles in one boiling pot. How can they be cleared and cooled? Much of what the ancient sages had to think about pertained to this. So it was that they set up the three studies of discipline, meditation, and knowledge, in order to control people so that they might be reformed and restored.

Nowadays younger students do not uphold the precepts, do not practice meditation, cultivate knowledge, and develop virtue. They just rely on wide learning and powerful intellect, acting in common, vulgar ways, so that they are impossible to reform. This is what I mean when I say that such talk is the bane of the Chan communities for ten thousand ages.

Only those lofty-minded people who travel on the correct basis, keeping sincere and faithful to understanding and clarifying the issue of life and death, will not be dragged in by this type. They say that such talk cannot be believed in and is like poisonous bird droppings, like water drunk and passed by a viper. It is not good even to read or hear of such talk, much less ingest it, for it will undoubtedly kill people. Those who know will naturally stay far away from it.

letter to Caotang

163.
Gifts of Teaching

It is related that the Chan master Wanan was frugal and austere, and used extemporaneous discussions and general talks for offerings. Among the monks of the community there were some who criticized him for this.

Hearing of this, Wanan said, "Dining on fine food in the

morning and disliking coarse fare in the evening is ordinary human feeling. Since you people have your minds on the magnitude of the matter of life and death, and have sought out an island of peace and solitude, you should be thinking of how your practice of the Way is not yet accomplished and how far removed you are from the time of the sages. How can you be concerned with your covetous desires all the time?"

Collection of the True Herdsman

164.
A Chan Master

Wanan was humane and considerate, and he conducted himself with modesty and austerity. Whenever he spoke, his words were simple yet the meaning was profound. He studied widely and had a strong memory. He would pursue reason to its final conclusion, and did not stop on any account, or follow anything arbitrarily.

When he discussed a story, contemporary or ancient, it was like being there in person—to those who heard, it was as clear as seeing with their own eyes. Students used to say that a year of meditation was not as good as a day of listening to the master's talk.

Record of Things Heard

165.
Buddhahood in This Life

Wanan said to the community assembly chief Bian:

My spiritual grandfather Yuanwu said, "Among the Chan folk of present times, few have fidelity and integrity, and none have humility. Many of the Confucians therefore slight them.

"Someday you might not avoid acting like this, so always act within the basis of the rules, do not run after power and gain or curry favor with people.

"Life, death, calamity, or trouble—let them all be, and you enter the realm of buddhahood without leaving the realm of demons."

Sermons

166.
Casual Attire

Assembly Chief Bian became leader and teacher of the community at a certain monastery on the holy Mount Lu. He always carried a bamboo staff and wore straw sandals. When he went to another monastery, the abbot, a monk named Hunrong, scolded him for his appearance, saying, "A teacher is a model and a guide for others; how can you avoid demeaning yourself when you behave like this?"

Bian laughed and said, "In human life it is considered pleasant to do as one wishes. What blame is on me in this regard?" He took up a brush, wrote a verse, and left.

That verse said:

> Don't say I am destitute;
> When the body is destitute, the Way is not.
> These straw sandals are fierce as tigers,
> This staff is lively as a dragon.
> When thirsty, I drink the water of Chan,
> When hungry, I eat chestnut thorn balls.
> Folks with bronze skulls and iron foreheads
> Are all on my mountain.

When that abbot read this he was ashamed.

Moon Cave Collection

105

167.
Showboats

Master Bian said to Hunrong:

Statues of dragons cannot make rain; how can paintings of cakes satisfy hunger? Monks who have no real virtue within but outwardly rely on flowery cleverness are like leaky boats brightly painted—if you put manikins in them and set them on dry ground they look fine, but once they go into the rivers and lakes, into the wind and waves, are they not in danger?

Moon Cave Collection

168.
Personal Responsibility

Master Bian said:

The so-called chief elder teaches in the place of the Buddha. Essential to this is purification of oneself in dealing with the community, utmost honesty and sincerity in executing affairs, and care not to divide one's mind by choosing between gain and loss.

It is up to the individual to do this, so one should definitely act in this way. As for the matter of succeeding or otherwise, even the sages of old could not be sure—how can we force the issue?

Moon Cave Collection

169.
Uniforms

Master Bian said:

When Fozhi was abbot at Xichan monastery, the monks strove for uniformity. Shuian alone, by nature empty and peaceful, took care of his body with utmost simplicity. He stood out in the crowd because of his appearance, yet he never gave it the slightest thought.

Fozhi scolded him, saying, "How can you be so offbeat?"

Shuian said, "It is not that I would not like to have a uniform, it is just that I am poor and do not have the wherewithal to make it. Had I the money, I too would like to make one or two suits of fine raiment and join the club. But since I am poor I cannot do anything about it."

Fozhi laughed at this. He knew Shuian could not be forced, so he let the matter drop.

Moon Cave Collection

170.
The Discipline of Awareness

Master Fozhi said:

A swift horse can run fast, but does not dare to gallop freely because of the bit and halter. When petty people, while obstinate and belligerent, do not indulge their feelings, it is because of punishments and laws. When the flow of consciousness does not dare to cling to objects, this is the power of awareness.

If students have no awareness and are unreflective, they are like fast horses with no bit and bridle, like petty people without law. With what can they put an end to greed and craving and quell errant thoughts?

instructions to a layman

171.
Four Limbs of Leadership

Fozhi said to Shuian:

The body of leadership has four limbs: enlightenment

107

and virtue, speech and action, humaneness and justice, etiquette and law. Enlightenment and virtue are the root of the teaching; humaneness and justice are the branches of the teaching. With no root, it is impossible to stand; with no branches it is impossible to be complete.

The ancient sages saw that students could not govern themselves, so they set up communities to settle them, and established leadership to direct them. Therefore the honor of the community is not for the leader, the plenitude of the necessities of life is not for the students—all of it is for the Way of enlightenment.

Therefore a good leader should honor first enlightenment and virtue, and be careful in speech and action. To be able to be a student, one should think first of goodness and right, and follow etiquette and law.

Thus the leadership could not stand but for the students, and the students cannot develop without the leadership. The leadership and the students are like the body and the arms, like the head and the feet. When great and small accord without opposition, they go by means of each other.

Therefore it is said, "Students keep the communities, the communities keep virtue." If the leadership has not virtue, then that community is on the verge of decline.

True Record

172.
Thinking of Trouble

Master Shuian said:

The Book of Changes says, "An ideal person thinks of trouble and prevents it." Therefore people of ancient times thought of the great trouble of birth and death, and prevented it with the Way, until eventually the Way waxed great and was transmitted for a long time.

People nowadays think that the vast distances of the search for the Way do not compare to the urgent immediacy of material interests. Because of this they vie in their habits of useless extravagance, calculating down to a hair tip, keeping an eye on everything that passes in front of them, with opportunistic plans in their hearts.

Therefore none can serve as guides for the whole year round, much less for considerations of life and death. This is why students are getting worse day by day, the communities are degenerating day by day, their unifying principles decline day by day, until they have reached a state of prostration from which they can hardly be saved. We must be aware.

True Record of Twin Forests

173.
A Direct Shortcut

Shuian said:

In the old days when I was traveling in search of the Way, I saw Gaoan at an evening assembly. He said, "The ultimate Way is a direct shortcut not akin to human sentiments. Essentially you must make your heart sincere and your mind true. Do not be a servant of ostentation or partiality. Ostentation is near to deception, and when you are partial you are imbalanced—neither of these is meet for the ultimate Way."

I reflected on these words to myself, approached their reason, and then made up my mind to put them into practice. Then when I saw Fozhi, who was to become my teacher, for the first time my mind was opened up by great insight. Only then was I able to live up to the aspiration of my life pilgrimage.

letter to Yuetang

109

174.
Nipping in the Bud

Shuian said:

Wherever Yuetang was leader of a Chan community, he made the practice of the Way his own responsibility. He did not send out fundraisers, nor did he go visiting grandees. For the year's food he would just use what was obtained from the monastery property. He refused many monks who wished to go preach for alms.

Some said, "The Buddha instructed the mendicants to take their bowls and beg to support physical life—how can you stop them and not permit it?"

Yuetang said, "In the Buddha's day it was all right, but I am afraid if we do it today there will be those who are fond of gain, to the point where they will wind up selling themselves."

So I think that Yuetang's nipping in the bud was profoundly cutting and brilliantly clear. His realistic words are still in my ears. As I look upon the present day in this way, has it not gone even further than people selling themselves?

Sermons

175.
A Thousand Days of Effort

Shuian said:

When the ancient worthies held leadership, they included themselves in carrying out the Way, never for a moment remiss or self-indulgent. In olden times the great Chan master Fenyang used to lament how deficient the imitation age was, and how students were difficult to teach, but his distinguished disciple Ciming said, "It is very easy—the trouble is that the teaching masters cannot guide well, that is all."

Fenyang said, "The ancients were pure and sincere, yet it was twenty or thirty years before they were successful in their accomplishment."

Ciming said, "This is not the talk of a sage philosopher. For someone who proceeds along the Path well, it is a matter of a thousand days of effort."

Some did not listen, saying that Ciming was talking nonsense.

Now the region where he worked was extremely cold, so Fenyang stopped the customary evening gathering. A foreign monk said to Fenyang (one version of the story has it that an Indian monk said this to him in a dream), "There are six great heroes in this assembly—why do you not teach?"

Before three years had passed, there were actually six people in Fenyang's group who realized enlightenment.

West Lake Annals

176.
Trading Off

Shuian said:

Recently we see leaders in various places with mind tricks to control their followers, while their followers serve the leaders with ulterior motives of influence, power, and profit. The leaders and followers trade off, above and below fooling each other. How can education prosper and communities flourish?

a letter

177.
Moving People

Shuian advised a disciple invited to speak at court:

To move people with words it is essential to be true and

111

cutting. If your words are not true and to the point, the reaction they evoke will be shallow—who would take them to heart?

In olden times our spiritual ancestor Baiyun, sending his disciple Wuzu, our spiritual great-grandfather, to a teaching assignment, carefully admonished him in these terms:

"The Chan Way is in decline, and is in danger, like eggs piled up. Do not indulge in negligence and irresponsibility. That uselessly kills time and also undermines ultimate virtue. You should be easygoing and broad-minded, assess proper measures. Help people, thinking of the whole community. Bring out the truth to pay back your debt to the enlightened ones and spiritual forebears."

Who would not have been moved on hearing this?

You have recently been summoned to speak before the imperial court. This is truly auspicious for the teaching. You must humble yourself in honor of the Way, make help and salvation your heart. Do not cut yourself down by pride.

Since antiquity the sages have been modest and gentle, respectful and circumspect. They preserved themselves with complete virtue and did not consider authority or rank to be glorious. In this way they were able to purify a time, their fame resounding beautifully for ten thousand generations.

I think my days are not long, and we will not meet in person ever again. That is the reason for this urgent admonition.

letter to Touzi

178.
A Retirement

Shuian was extraordinary from youth, and had great determination. He valued character and integrity, he did not go in for foolish waste, he did not pursue petty criticism. He was broad-minded and openhearted. He put principles into practice in his actual behavior. Even when calamity and trouble were happening at once, he was never seen to be downcast.

Shuian was abbot at eight public monasteries in four cities. Wherever he went he toiled and labored with the establishment of practice of the Way at heart.

In 1178 he retired from Pure Kindness monastery on West Lake. He wrote:

> Six years of sprinkling and sweeping temples in the
>   imperial capital;
> Tiles and pebbles turn into celestial chambers.
> Today the palace is done, and I return;
> A pure wind rises on all sides from the staff.

The gentry and commonfolk tried to get him to stay there, but he would not. He sailed a small boat up to Heavenly Brightness monastery in Longwater prefecture. Before long he appeared to be ill, took leave of the assembly, and announced his end.

biography

179.

The Derelict Age

Yuetang said:

In ancient times Baizhang, Chan Master of Great Wisdom, concerned about the haughtiness and laziness of monks of the age of dereliction, drew up special rules and guidelines to prevent this. According to capacity and potential, each was given a responsibility.

The leader lived in a ten-foot-square room, and the community lived in a common hall, arrayed in a strict order, with ten assembly chiefs. It was ordered like the civil government: the leaders brought up the essentials of the teaching, the subordinates took care of the many aspects of it, causing above and below to understand one another, like the body using the arms, the arms using the fingers—everyone followed.

Therefore those of our predecessors who followed this tradition and received its help and worked carefully to carry it out could do so because the remaining influence of the sages of old had not died out.

Recently we see the Chan communities declining and changing. The students value talent and demean perseverance in practice, they like the ephemeral and the ostentatious and slight the true and the simple. Over the days and months they get into a decadent trend.

At first it is just taking things easy for a time, but after long indulgence and habituation people think it is natural to be this way, and do not consider it wrong or contrary to principle.

Now the leader timidly fears the subordinates, while the subordinates keep a watchful eye on the superior. When the leader is relaxed the subordinates speak sweetly and grovel for favor, but when they find an opening they scheme treacherously to encompass his downfall. Those who win are considered wise and those who lose are considered foolish—they no longer question the order of nobility and meanness, or the principles of right and wrong. What one has done, another will imitate; what is said below is followed above, what is done before is continued after.

Unless teachers of great sagacity mount the power of will

114

and pile up a hundred years of effective work, this decadence and stagnation cannot be reformed.

letter to Master Shun

180.
Watering Melons at Midday

Yuetang held leadership longest at Pure Kindness monastery. Someone said to him, "You have been practicing the Way here for years, but I have never heard that you have had any successors among your disciples. Are you not letting your teacher down?"

Yuetang did not reply.

Another day that person repeated the question, and Yuetang said, "Have you not heard of the story of the man in ancient times who planted melons? He liked melons very much, and he watered them at midday in midsummer. As a result, the melons rotted where they lay.

"What does this mean? It is not that his liking for the melons was not earnest, but that his watering was not timely, and by that he ruined them.

"Old teachers in various places support monks without observing whether their work on the Way is fulfilled within them, or if their capacity is broad and far-reaching. They just want to speed up their careers, but when you carefully examine their morals, they are corrupt, and when you look into their words and actions, they are contradictory. What they call impartial and correct is biased and prejudicial.

"Is this not a matter of liking that goes beyond measure? This is just like watering melons at midday. I am deeply afraid the knowing would laugh, so I do not do it."

North Mountain Annals

115

181.
A Testimonial

Xuetang said:

Astronomer Huang Luzhi once said, "Chan Master Huanglong Huinan was profound in mind and generous in consideration, and he was not influenced by any thing or being. In all his life he never had any pretentions. Among his disciples there were those who had never seen him joyful or angry in his life. He treated everyone with equal sincerity, even servants and workers. Therefore he was able to cause the way of Ciming to flourish without raising his voice or changing his expression. This was not without reason."

engraved on a stone at Huanglong

182.
A Demonstration

Yuetang said:

In 1129, when Zhong Xiang rebelled in Liyang, Chan Master Wenshu Dao was in danger. When the power of the rebels had grown to full force, his disciples fled, but the master said, "Can calamity be avoided?" Thus remaining resolutely in his room, the master was eventually killed by plunderers.

The lay disciple Wugou wrote an afterword to the collection of the master's sayings:

"Liking life and disliking death is the ordinary feeling for human beings. Only the complete human beings realize they are originally unborn, and while alive have no attachment, and comprehend that they never perish, so though they die they have no fear. Therefore they can face the times of tribulation of death and birth without wavering in their determination.

116

"The master was one such person. Because the master's enlightened virtue and fidelity to truth were worthy to teach the communities and set an example for later generations, therefore he was entitled Zhengdao, True Guide. He was a successor of Chan Master Fojian."

Records of Great Master Hui of Lushan

183.

A Diagnosis

Master Xinwen Fen said:

Many are the monks who develop sickness because of Chan. Those whose sickness is in their eyes and ears think staring and glaring, inclining the ear and nodding, are Chan. Those whose sickness is in the mouth and tongue think crazy talk and wild shouting are Chan. Those whose sickness is in their hands and feet think walking back and forth and pointing east and west are Chan. Those whose sickness is in their hearts and guts think that investigating the mystery, studying the marvel, transcending feelings, and detaching from views are Chan.

Speaking from the standpoint of reality, all of these are sicknesses. Only a true teacher can clearly discern the subtle indications, knowing at a glance if people understand or not, discerning whether they have arrived or not, the moment they enter the door.

After that, using awl and needle, the teacher frees them from subtle entrapments, bears down on their sticking points, tests whether they are true or false, and determines if they are bogus or genuine, all this without sticking to one method or being unaware of when to change and pass on, to cause them

117

eventually to walk in the realm of peace, happiness, and freedom from care, before the teacher finally rests.

True Record

184.
The Blue Cliff Record

Xinwen said:

The Way that is specially transmitted outside of doctrine is utterly simple and quintessential. From the beginning there is no other discussion; our predecessors carried it out without doubt and kept it without deviation.

During the Tianxi era of the Song dynasty (1012–1022), the Chan master Xuedou, using his talents of eloquence and erudition, with beautiful ideas in kaleidoscopic display, seeking freshness and polishing skill, followed the example of Fenyang in making verses on ancient stories, to catch and control the students of the time. The manner of Chan went through a change from this point on.

Then during the Xuanho era (1119–1125) Yuanwu also set forth his own ideas on the stories and verses from Xuedou, and from then on the collection was known as *The Blue Cliff Record*. At that time, the perfectly complete masters of the age, like Wayfarer Ning, Huanglong Sixin, Lingyuan, and Fojian, could not contradict what he said, so new students of later generations prized his words and would recite them by day and memorize them by night, calling this the highest study. None realized this was wrong, and unfortunately students' meditational skills deteriorated.

In the beginning of the Shaoxing era (1131–1163), Yuanwu's enlightened successor Miaoxi went into eastern China and saw that the Chan students there were recalcitrant, pursuing the study of this book to such an extent that their involvement became an evil. So he broke up the woodblocks of *The Blue Cliff Record* and analyzed its explanations, thus to get rid of illusions and rescue those who were floundering, stripping away excess and setting aside exaggeration, demolishing the false and revealing the true, dealing with the text in a special way. Students gradually began to realize their error, and did not idolize it anymore.

So if not for Miaoxi's high illumination and far sight, riding on the power of the vow of compassion to save an age of dereliction from its ills, the Chan communities would be in peril.

letter to Zhang Zishao

185.
No Fixed Classes

Chan Master Choan said to Prime Minister Yu Yunwen:

The Great Way is clear and open—no one is originally either foolish or wise on the Way. It is like the case of certain ancients who started out plowing and fishing but became advisors to emperors—how could this be tried with fixed classes of intelligence?

However, it requires a certain personal power to participate.

Extensive Record

186.
Leadership Training

Choan said:

To train yourself to deal with the assembly, it is necessary to use wisdom. To dispel delusion and remove sentiments, you must first be aware. If you turn away from awareness and mix with the dusts, then your mind will be enshrouded. When wisdom and folly are not distinguished, matters get tangled up.

letter to a monastery superintendent

187.
Penetrating Obstruction by Reason

Choan said:

When Fojian was the leader of the Great Peace community, Gaoan was in charge of taking care of guests. Gaoan was young and high-spirited, and he looked down on everyone else, there being few who met with his approval.

One day at the time of the noon meal, as Gaoan sounded the call he saw a worker placing food before Fojian in a special vessel. Gaoan left the hall, announcing in a loud voice, "If the teacher of five hundred monks acts like this, how can he be an example for later students?"

Fojian pretended not to see or hear this.

Then when Fojian left the hall, Gaoan looked and found that the special vessel contained pickled vegetables, for it turned out that Fojian had a chronic stomach ailment and did not partake of oil, which was ordinarily used in the monastic food for nutrition.

Gaoan was ashamed, and went to the leader's room to announce his resignation.

Fojian said, "What you said was quite right. But it just happens that I am sick, that is all. I have heard that a sage said, "Penetrate all obstructions by reason." Because what I eat is not better, I am not doubted by the community. Your will and temper are clear and far-reaching; someday you will

120

be a cornerstone of the source teaching. Don't let this stick in your mind."

When Fojian moved, Gaoan went elsewhere, and later became a successor of Foyan.

188.
Teaching Government Officials

Choan said:

When discoursing on the Way to government officials, in dialogue you must strip away their intellectual understanding and not let them settle into clichés. It is just essential to purely clarify the one experience of transcendence.

The late teacher Miaoxi once said, "When you meet grandees, answer if they ask questions, otherwise refrain." And one must be such a person too, to be of assistance to the times on hearing such words, so as not to injure the body of living Buddhism.

letter to a Chan abbot

189.
The Peril of Leadership

Choan said:

Fine land nurtures beings well, a benevolent ruler nurtures people well. Nowadays many who are known as leaders do not take the people to heart, instead giving precedence to their own desires. They do not like hearing good words, and do like to cover up their faults, indulging in improper practices and vainly pleasing themselves for a time. When petty people take to the likes and dislikes of the leaders, is the path of leadership not in peril?

letter to a Chan elder

121

190.
Killed but Not Shamed

Choan said to Yean:

The Lay Master of the Purple Cliff said, "My former teacher Miaoxi makes virtue, integrity, and courage his priorities in everyday life. He can be befriended but not estranged, approached but not pressed, killed but not shamed. His abode is not extravagant, his food is not rich. He faces the troubles and problems of life and death as if they were nothing. He is truly an example of what is meant by the saying, 'The sword of the great smith is hard to clash with.' The only worry is unforeseen injury."

Ultimately it turned out as the lay master said.

Annals of Phantom Hermitage

191.
Choosing Assistants

Choan said:

As a leader, Ye-an comprehends the processes of the human mind and is aware of the great body of the community. He once said to me, "To be the host in a place you must choose people of determination and action for assistants. They are like a comb for hair, a mirror for a face—then what is beneficial and what is deleterious, what is fine and what is unseemly, cannot be hidden."

Annals of Phantom Hermitage

192.
Superficiality and Depth

Choan said:

Latter-day students are superficial, uselessly valuing their ears while slighting their eyes—ultimately none of them can fathom the profound mystery.

Therefore it is said, "No matter how high the mountain, on it are tiers of crags and clusters of bamboo; no matter how deep the ocean, in it are fonds and currents."

If you want to study the Great Way, the essence is in investigating its heights and depths. After that you can illumine the obscure subtleties, and adapt responsively with no limit.

letter to a Chan elder

193.
The Mind of Saints and Sages

Choan said to Cabinet Minister Yu:

The mind of saints and sages is tolerant and easygoing, still their reason is clear. They are serene and aloof, yet their deeds are evident.

Whatever they do, they do not expect hasty completion, and are willing to persevere long. They do not agree to insistence on advancement, but they approve of striving to approach the Way. Those who infer the will of saints and sages from this and then maintain it over a thousand generations will be thus.

Annals of Phantom Hermitage

194.
History Review

Cabinet Minister Yu said:

Before Bodhidharma, the founder of Chan, there was no such thing as the Chan abbacy, the institutionalization of the living exemplar of Buddhism. Bodhidharma's descendants, carrying out the Way in response to the world, were pressed and could not avoid this development, but still they lived in simple huts, enough for shelter from wind and rain, and took food enough to appease hunger. Suffering bitter hardships, they were haggard and emaciated; there were those who couldn't stand their misery, and kings and important men wanted to see them but could not. Therefore, all that they set up was free and unfettered, startling the heavens and shaking the earth.

In later generations they weren't like that. In high buildings, with spacious rooms, fine raiment and rich food, they got whatever they wanted. At this, the cohorts of the evil one began to greatly affect their minds; they lingered at the gates of temporal power, wagging their tails begging for pity, in extreme cases taking by trickery and usurping by status, like stealing gold in broad daylight, not knowing there is such a thing as cause and effect in the world.

The letters of Chan Master Miaoxi bring out everyone's current mental habits, not leaving so much as a wisp, like the legendary pond water that enables one to see the internal organs clearly. If you can receive them with faith and put them into practice, what's the need to specially seek Buddhism besides?

seen on a stone engraving

195.
The Revival of the Linji School of Chan

Cabinet Minister Yu said to Choan:

In the old days Miaoxi revived the Way of Linji in the autumn of its withering and decline; but by nature he esteemed humility and emptiness. He never flaunted or advertised his insight and reason, and never in his life did he run to people of authority and power, and he did not grab profit and support.

Miaoxi once said, "Myriad affairs cannot be accomplished by taking it easy, nor can they be maintained with a haughty attitude. It seems that there is that which is beneficial to the times and helpful to the people, and that which is in error and has no merit. If you indulge the latter and haughtily take it easy, then you will fail." I have taken these words to heart, and they have become a lesson for my whole life.

records of an attendant

196.
Custom

Chan Master Mian said:

The rise and decline of Chan communities is in their conduct and principles; the refinement or badness of students is in their customs and habits. Even if the ancients lived in nests and caves, drinking from streams and eating from the trees, to practice this in the present would not be suitable. Even if people of the present dress and eat richly, to practice this in ancient times would not have been suitable. Is it anything else but a matter of habituation?

What people see day and night as the ordinary, they inevitably think everything in the world should properly be that way. One day when they are driven to give this up and go to something else, they not only doubt and disbelieve, they probably will not go along.

When things are considered in this light, it is clear that people feel secure in what they are used to, and are startled by what they have never witnessed. This is their ordinary condition, so why wonder about it?

letter to Councillor Shi

197.
The Good and the Corrupt

Mian said:

My late teacher Yingan used to say, "The good and the corrupt are opposite—we cannot but distinguish them. The good maintain truth, virtue, benevolence, and justice to take their stand. The corrupt are devoted to power and profit, and do things by flattery and deception.

"The good accomplish their will and always put into practice what they learn. The corrupt, occupying rank, mostly indulge their selfishness, jealous of the intelligent and envious of the able; they indulge their cravings and grasp for material possessions, and there is no telling how far they will go.

"Therefore, when there are good people there, a community flourishes; and when corrupt people are employed, then the community declines. If there is even one corrupt person present, it is surely impossible for there to be peace and tranquility."

letter to a teacher

198.
Three Don'ts

Mian said:

In leadership there are three don'ts: when there is much to do, don't be afraid; when there is nothing to do, don't be hasty; and don't talk about opinions of right and wrong.

126

A leader who succeeds in these three things won't be confused or deluded by external objects.

an attendant's record

199.
Wolves in Sheep's Clothing

Mian said:
When mendicants whose conduct in everyday life is bad and who have a history of being no good are known as such in the community, this is not worrisome; but when those who are inwardly not good are called sages by the people, that is truly worrisome.

a letter

200.
The Revealing Mirror of Truth

Mian said to Shuian:
When people revile you, you should accept it docilely. One should not lightly hear the words of others and then arbitrarily set forth narrow views. For the most part, opportunistic flatterers have cliques, perverted cleverness has many methods: those with prejudice in their hearts like to publicize their private wishes, and those who create jealousy and envy unilaterally negate common discussion and consensus.

On the whole, the aims of these people are narrow and restricted, their vision is dim and short, they think those with individualistic differences must be extraordinary and consider those who undermine open discussion to be outstanding.

However, as long as you know that what you are doing is right after all, and the vilification itself is in them, then over a long time it will become clear of itself; you don't have to specially say it, and you don't have to insist on your rightness and offend people.

a letter

201.
Making Choices

Master Zide Hui said:

In general, when people are sincere and headed in the right direction, they can still be employed even if they are dull. If they are flatterers with ulterior motives, they are ultimately harmful even if they are smart.

On the whole, if their psychological orientation is not correct, people are unworthy of establishment in positions of service and leadership even if they have talent and ability.

letter to Master Jiantang

202.
Loss of Order

Zide said:

The Chan Master of Great Wisdom Baizhang Huaihai, (720–814, one of the founders of the Chan commune system) specially established pure rules to help save mendicants in the age of spiritual dereliction from the corruption into which they had fallen. Thenceforth the sages of the past followed and applied them, carrying them out seriously in practice. There was teaching, there was order, there was consistency.

At the end of the Shaoxing era (ca. 1160), there were still mature people in the communities who could keep the traditional laws and didn't presume to depart from them for a minute. In recent years they have lost the order of the school, and the fabric of the order is dissolute or incoherent.

Therefore it is said, "Lift up one net and a multitude of eyes open; neglect one opportunity and myriad affairs collapse." It has just about gotten to where the order is no longer working and the communities are no longer flourishing.

But the ancients embodied the fundamental, whereby they made the outgrowths straight. They just worried that the measures of the teaching were not strictly kept rather than worrying that students wouldn't reach where they were.

What they considered right was right in its impartiality, but leaders in various places nowadays mix partiality in with impartiality, using the outgrowths to direct the root. Those above like wealth without practicing the Way, while those below covet wealth without practicing duty. When above and below are confused and disordered, guest and host are mixed up, how can we have the wearers of the patched garment turn toward truth and have the communities flourish?

letter to Minister Yu

203.
Making Distinctions

Zide said:

Before a fine jade is cut, it is the same as tile or stone; before a good steed is raced, it is mixed in with nags. When cut and polished, raced and tested, then jade and stone, charger and nag, are distinguished.

Now mendicants with sagacity and virtue have not yet been employed, they are mixed in with the crowd. Ultimately how can they be distinguished?

It is essential that highly perceptive people be elected by

129

public consensus, entrusted with the affairs of office, tested for talent and ability, judged by accomplishment of tasks. Thus they will prove to be far different from the mediocre.

letter to Huoan

204.
Selecting Buddhas

Master Huoan Ti first studied with Si-an Yuan Budai at Huguo monastery on the famous and holy Mount Tiantai. In an address in the teaching hall, Si-an quoted Layman Pang's verse on "Selection of Buddhas." When he came to the line "This is the place for selecting buddhas," Si-an shouted. At that moment Huoan was greatly enlightened.

He composed a verse on his realization:

Where the assessment culminates, you see the subject;
At the end of the road, you enter the examination place.
Pick up a hairtip—wind and rain are swift
No graduation party this time.

After this he secluded himself on Mount Tiantai. The deputy premier, Mr. Qian, admired his character, and insisted that he respond to the needs of the world by becoming a public teacher at a certain monastery. When Huoan heard of this, he said, "I can't hang out mutton and sell dog flesh," and disappeared in the night.

205.
Recognition

In the beginning of the Jiandao era (1165–1174), Xiatang was resident master at a public monastery when he saw Huoan's eulogy on a portrait of Yuantong:

130

Not resting on the fundamental, he disturbs sentient
    beings
Looking up at him, gazing on him, with eyes as if blind.
The scenery of the Capital City extends through all
    time—
Who walks groping along a wall?

Xiatang was startled and delighted. He said, "I didn't think
Si-an had such successors." Then Xiatang looked for Huoan
all over and finally found him in Jiangxin. He invited him
from among the crowd to fill the position of the first in the
assembly.

Rustic Annals of Tiantai

206.
Fulfillment of Conditions

In the beginning of the Jiandao era, Huoan drifted over
to see Xiatang at Tiger Hill, where the monastics and lay folk
of the metropolitan area heard of his lofty manner, prompting
them to go to the prefectural capital to nominate him to be
resident teacher at Jiaobao temple in the city.

When Huo-an heard of this, he said, "My late teacher Si-
an instructed me, 'Another day, meeting old age, stay.' Now
it seems that this has been fulfilled." So he gladly answered
the request to stay there. It turned out that the old name of
Jiaobao temple was Laoshouan, Old Age Hermitage.

Tiger Hill Annals

207.
An Impromptu Talk

After Huoan had entered Jiaobao temple, a patron re-
quested him to give an impromptu talk.

He said, "The Way is constant and unchanging; things

131

deteriorate and must change. In ancient times the great Chan masters took lessons from the study of antiquity, considering what was appropriate or not, holding by the middle way, working to unify people's minds, with enlightenment as the guide. That is why their simple manner, cool as ice, has not disappeared to this very day.

"In terms of the Chan school, even getting understanding before anything is said still cramps the manner of our religion, and even discerning clearly on hearing a phrase buries the enlightened ones.

"Even though it is so, 'Going, I reach the water's end; sitting, I watch when the clouds rise.' "

Thenceforth monks, nuns, and lay folk rejoiced in what they had never heard before, and a veritable city of people took refuge with him.

208.
Governing Wild Foxes

Once Huoan was teaching publicly, gentry and common people came in droves to take refuge with him. A mendicant relayed this to Tiger Hill, where Xiatang said, "That mountain savage is using blind man's Chan to govern that bunch of wild fox ghosts."

When Huoan heard of this, he replied with a poem:

You may dislike a mountain savage
Leading a group, guiding an order, as though without
    doing so
Transcending convention, holding up a broom handle
    upside down
Blind man's Chan governs the wild fox monks.

Xiatang just laughed.

Record of Things Heard

209.
Balancing

Huoan said to Minister of State Ceng Tai:

The essential point in studying the Way is like balancing stones to weigh things: just get them even, that is all—it won't work if one side is too heavy. Pushing ahead and lagging behind are both the same in being one-sided. When you realize this you can study the way.

a letter

210.
Talent and Capacity

Chan Master Xiatang Yuan said to Huoan:

People's talent and capacity are naturally great or small, for these things cannot be taught. Those whose paper is small cannot wrap up large objects; those whose rope is short cannot draw from a deep well. An owl can catch a louse and see a hair by night, but when the sun comes out in daytime, it irritates the owl's eyes so much that it cannot even see a hill. It seems that the distribution is set.

Annals of Tiger Hill

211.
A Moment in History

Chan Master Jiantang Ji lived on Mount Guan in Fanyang for some twenty years, making soup of wild herbs and millet for his meals; he had utterly severed his mind from glory and success.

Once when he went down the mountain he heard the sound of weeping by the road. Feeling pity, Jiantang went to

133

inquire. It turned out that there was a whole family cold and sick; two members of the family had just died, and they were so poor they had nothing in which to put the bodies.

Jiantang made a special trip to town to obtain coffins to bury them.

Everyone in the village was moved.

The minister, Mr. Li, said to the grandees, "Old Ji of our locality is a mendicant imbued with the Way; he bestows kindness as well as material goods. How can we let him stay forever on Mount Guan?"

At that time Military Inspector Wang, who was making a tour of the various highways, reported this in Jiujiang, and the district governor, Mr. Lin Shuda, had the teaching seat at Yuantong vacated and invited Jiantang there.

When Jiantang heard this order, he said, "My Way is going into effect," and gladly took up his staff and went there. To expound the Teaching, he said, "Yuantong doesn't open a fresh herb shop—to each I just sell a dead cat head. I don't know who doesn't think or figure—upon partaking the whole body runs with cold sweat."

The monastics and lay people were startled and considered this unusual. This teaching center now flourished greatly.

Records of Lazy Hermitage

212.
Sharing

Jiantang said:

When the people of old cultivated themselves and conquered their minds, they shared the Way with others. When they undertook tasks and accomplished works, they shared the achievement with others. When the Way was accomplished and achievement revealed, they shared the fame with others. This is why nothing in the Way was not clear, no accomplishment was not consummated, no fame was not glorious.

People nowadays are not like that. They are exclusively concerned about their own ways, and just worry that others will surpass them. Also they cannot pursue the good and work for what is right, because they are aggrandizing themselves. Concentrating on their own achievement, they don't want others to have it.

Also they cannot trust in the wise or get along with the able, because they magnify themselves. They are solely concerned with their own fame, not sharing it with others. They cannot guide people with humility, because they consider themselves successful.

Therefore this Path cannot avoid obscurity, their achievement cannot avoid loss, their fame cannot avoid dishonor. This is the great distinction between students of ancient and modern times.

213.
Growth

Jiantang said:

Studying the Way is like planting a tree—if you cut it just when it branches out, it can be used for firewood; if you cut it when it's about to reach full growth, it can be used for rafters; if you cut it when it's somewhat stronger, it can be used for beams; and if you cut if when it's old and huge, it can be used for pillars.

Could it not be that when you take the attainment over the long run the profit is greater?

Therefore the people of old saw to it that their Way was

sure and great and not narrow, their determination and will was far-reaching and profound and not shortsighted, and their words were lofty and not mean.

Although they met with the contradictions of the times and experienced the extremes of starvation and cold, perishing in the mountains and valleys, because of the residual power of their bequest, spanning hundreds and thousands of years, people of later times still transmit it as religious law.

If in the past they had been narrow in their Way, opportunistic in admitting people, seeking rapprochement for immediate ambitions, talking slavishly, serving authority, their profit would have ended at glory in one lifetime. How could there have been enrichment left over to reach later generations?

letter to Prime Minister Li

214.
A Successor to the Ancients

Mr. Wu, the imperial official, said to Jiantang:

The ancients calmed their minds and obliterated their self-consciousness in mountains and valleys, drinking from streams and eating from trees, in the manner of those who have absolutely no thought of success and fame. Yet the time came when they were called upon by emperors.

They hid their light and concealed their tracks in the mills and at other menial chores. From the beginning they had no thought of glory or achievement, in the end they stood in the ranks of the transmitters of the lamp.

Therefore, when attained in unminding, the Path is great and the virtue universal; when sought with ambition, the fame is ignoble and the aspiration narrow.

But your measure and capacity are stable and far-reaching, succeeding in the footsteps of the ancients. Thus you could live on Mount Guan for seventeen years and finally become a good vessel of truth in the community.

Monks of the present have nothing to concentrate on within, while outside they pursue distracting frills. They have little foresight, and no sense of the great body. Therefore they cannot help spiritual teaching, and thus they are a long way from you.

Recollections of Attendant Gao

215.
The Ordinary Condition of Human Beings

Jiantang said:

It is the ordinary condition of human beings that few are able to be free from delusion. Usually they are enshrouded by their beliefs, obstructed by their doubts, slighted by their contempt, drowned by their likes.

Once belief is biased, when people hear words they do not think about truth, until eventually it comes to words that exceed what is appropriate. When doubt is extreme, people do not listen to words even if they are true, until there is hearing that misses truth.

When people disrespect others, they lose sight of their worthy qualities. When people like something, they will keep around those who should be abandoned. These are all indulgence in private feelings without considering reason, eventually forgetting the Way of enlightened ones, losing the heart of the community.

So what ordinary feelings take lightly is what sages take seriously. An ancient worthy said, "Those who plan for what is ahead first check what is near at hand. Those who strive for the great must be careful about the small."

It should be a matter of a wide range of choice and careful use therein; it is surely not a matter of admiring the high and liking the unusual.

letter to Mr. Wu

216.
A Chan Master

Jiantang was pure and clear, and even-minded. He reached people with kindness and benevolence. If students made small mistakes, he would cover for them and protect them to develop their virtue. He once said of this, "Who has no faults? Excellence is a matter of reforming them."

When Jiantang was living on Mount Guan in Fanyang, once in the dead of winter it rained and snowed continuously so long that he ran out of food, yet the master behaved as if he weren't aware of it. He made a poem on this occasion that said:

> The hearth's without fire, the knapsack empty,
> The snow is like apricot blossoms falling at year's end.
> Patch robe over my head, burning scraps of wood,
> I am not conscious of my body in peaceful quietude.
> In daily life I go on the Way by myself,
> Not rushing after glory and fame.

On the day he answered the request to be teaching master of Yuantong monastery on holy Mount Lu, he came with only a staff and straw sandals. Those who saw him looked refreshed and felt relieved. The governor of the Nine Rivers region, Mr. Lin Shuda, said when he saw him. "This is a bridge of Buddhism."

Thenceforth his name was honored in all quarters. His behavior truly had the character of the masters of old. On the day he died, even the monastery servants and workers wept.

138

Shambhala Classics

Appreciate Your Life: The Essence of Zen Practice, by Taizan Maezumi Roshi.

The Art of Peace, by Morihei Ueshiba. Edited by John Stevens.

The Art of War, by Sun Tzu. Translated by the Denma Translation Group.

The Art of Worldly Wisdom, by Baltasar Gracián. Translated by Joseph Jacobs.

Awakening to the Tao, by Liu I-ming. Translated by Thomas Cleary.

Bodhisattva of Compassion: The Mystical Tradition of Kuan Yin, by John Blofeld.

The Book of Five Rings, by Miyamoto Musashi. Translated by Thomas Cleary.

The Book of Tea, by Kakuzo Okakura.

Breath by Breath: The Liberating Practice of Insight Meditation, by Larry Rosenberg.

Cutting Through Spiritual Materialism, by Chögyam Trungpa.

The Diamond Sutra and The Sutra of Hui-neng. Translated by Wong Mou-lam and A. F. Price.

The Essential Teachings of Zen Master Hakuin. Translated by Norman Waddell.

For the Benefit of All Beings, by H.H. the Dalai Lama. Translated by the Padmakara Translation Group.

The Great Path of Awakening, by Jamgön Kongtrül. Translated by Ken McLeod.

Insight Meditation: A Psychology of Freedom, by Joseph Goldstein.

The Japanese Art of War: Understanding the Culture of Strategy, by Thomas Cleary.

Kabbalah: The Way of the Jewish Mystic, by Perle Epstein.

Lovingkindness: The Revolutionary Art of Happiness, by Sharon Salzberg.

Meditations, by J. Krishnamurti.

Monkey: A Journey to the West, by David Kherdian.

The Myth of Freedom and the Way of Meditation, by Chögyam Trungpa.

Narrow Road to the Interior: And Other Writings, by Matsuo Bashō. Translated by Sam Hamill.

The Places That Scare You: A Guide to Fearlessness in Difficult Times, by Pema Chödrön.

The Rumi Collection: An Anthology of Translations of Mevlâna Jalâluddin Rumi. Edited by Kabir Helminski.

Seeking the Heart of Wisdom: The Path of Insight Meditation, by Joseph Goldstein and Jack Kornfield.

Seven Taoist Masters: A Folk Novel of China. Translated by Eva Wong.

Shambhala: The Sacred Path of the Warrior, by Chögyam Trungpa.

Siddhartha, by Hermann Hesse. Translated by Sherab Chödzin Kohn.

The Spiritual Teaching of Ramana Maharshi, by Ramana Maharshi.

Start Where You Are: A Guide to Compassionate Living, by Pema Chödrön.

T'ai Chi Classics. Translated with commentary by Waysun Liao.

Tao Teh Ching, by Lao Tzu. Translated by John C. H. Wu.

The Taoist I Ching, by Liu I-ming. Translated by Thomas Cleary.

The Tibetan Book of the Dead: The Great Liberation through Hearing in the Bardo. Translated with commentary by Francesca Fremantle and Chögyam Trungpa.

Training the Mind and Cultivating Loving-Kindness, by Chögyam Trungpa.

The Tree of Yoga, by B. K. S. Iyengar.

The Way of a Pilgrim and The Pilgrim Continues His Way. Translated by Olga Savin.

The Way of the Bodhisattva, by Shantideva. Translated by the Padmakara Translation Group.

When Things Fall Apart: Heart Advice for Difficult Times, by Pema Chödrön.

The Wisdom of No Escape: And the Path of Loving-Kindness, by Pema Chödrön.

The Wisdom of the Prophet: Sayings of Muhammad. Translated by Thomas Cleary.

The Yoga-Sūtra of Patañjali: A New Translation with Commentary. Translated by Chip Hartranft.

Zen Lessons: The Art of Leadership. Translated by Thomas Cleary.

Zen Training: Methods and Philosophy, by Katsuki Sekida.